Cognition in Emotion

Consciousness Literature & the Arts 10

General Editor:
Daniel Meyer-Dinkgräfe

Editorial Board:
Anna Bonshek, Per Brask, John Danvers,
William S. Haney II, Amy Ione,
Michael Mangan, Arthur Versluis,
Christopher Webster, Ralph Yarrow

Cognition in Emotion
An Investigation through Experiences with Art

TONE ROALD

Rodopi

Amsterdam - New York, NY 2007

Cover image: detail of *Like is Only Known by Alike* by Anne Thorseth, 2000, with kind permission of the artist

Cover Design: Aart Jan Bergshoeff

The paper on which this book is printed meets the requirements of "ISO 9706:1994, Information and documentation - Paper for documents - Requirements for permanence".

ISBN: 978-90-420-2333-8
ISSN: 1573-2193
©Editions Rodopi B.V., Amsterdam - New York, NY 2007
Printed in the Netherlands

Table of Content

Acknowledgements

Many people have been directly involved in the production of this book, and I would like to take this opportunity to express my gratitude. I would like to thank my husband, Thomas Collier, who left his mark on every page and was present on every day that it took me to gather my thoughts and words for this book. I would also like to acknowledge my two mentors: Bjarne Sode Funch, who so aptly communicates in matters of art and life, and whose generosity and integrity remain a source of inspiration, and Simo Køppe, who so eloquently shares his scholarly aplomb and thoroughgoing knowledge of psychology. Moreover, I would like to extend my thanks to Esbjerg Museum of Art for helping facilitate this research as well as to all the interviewees, who gave generously of their time and experience. Thanks also to Andreas Roald and Jonna Clæsøe for helping with the layout, and to Dina Haffar, Morten Jørgensen, Sofie Nielsen and Ann Kathrin Storenes for commenting on various parts of the book. The cover image, 'Like is Only Known by Alike' (detail), is used with the kind permission of Anne Thorseth, and the image of 'Downward Trend' is used with the kind permission of Nina Saunders. Thank you both. I would also like to extend my thanks to all other family and friends. This book is dedicated to my mother, Aud Judith.

Introduction

If you can conceive yourself, if possible, suddenly stripped of all the emotion with which our world now inspires you, and try to imagine it as it exists, purely by itself, without your favorable or unfavorable, hopeful or apprehensive comment...No one portion of the universe would then have importance beyond another; and the whole character of its things and series of its events would be without significance, character, expression, or perspective.

William James
The Varieties of Religious Experience (1893, p. 147).

With these words, William James, one of the founding forces of modern psychology, asserts the centrality of emotions in human experience – without emotions there is nothing but a void of insignificance, no experience of colour and meaning, no guide to our actions. Such statements are not new, and similar proclamations have been made countless times throughout history by artists, philosophers and other psychologists. Artistic traditions have constantly wrestled with questions relating to emotions, such as their influence on human relations, the way they interact with each other and how they define us as human beings. Emotions appear as essential ingredients in most human actions and interactions, facilitating the brightest and darkest in human conduct. Their significance is evident, as one most often remembers events that are rich in emotional content and not merely the humdrum happenings. Emotional instability also leads to much suffering and is a pervasive aspect of many mental disorders. Emotions are vital to a wide array of human experiences and contribute to their unique qualities (Dolan 2002).

In this book, various forms of emotions are explored because, although the importance of emotions seems obvious, their nature appears elusive. Numerous positions exist to this enigma and to divine the nature of emotion is proving a complex and extensive task. One main position, for instance, holds that emotions are animalistic, brute impulses, largely without association to reason (a Neo-Stoic view currently held by e.g. Cosmides and Tooby, 2000, 2006; see also Nussbaum 2001). Proponents of this position contend accordingly that emotions need to be thoroughly restricted by thought so that fully rational and, thereby, useful citizens will emerge. Conversely, others propose that emotions are immersed in acumen and intelligence, are springs of profound consciousness and knowledge, with importance for daily orientation and conduct, and for the development of ethics and morale (e.g. Ben-Ze'ev 2000; Nussbaum 2001). This contemporary emotion conundrum can be traced back to the ancient Greeks: Plato suggested in *The Republic* that the soul is tripartite, containing cognition, motivation and emotion as distinct features. Aristotle argued the impossibility of such disparate phenomena and for a closer integration between these three notions (Nussbaum 2001). He reasoned that cognition is necessary for an emotional response and wrote:

> The Emotions are all those feelings that so change men as to affect their judgements, and that are also attended by pain or pleasure. Such are anger, pity, fear and the like, with their opposites. We must arrange what we have to say about each of them under three heads. Take, for instance, the emotion of anger: here we must discover (1) what the state of mind of angry people is, (2) who the people are with whom they usually get angry, and (3) on what grounds they are angry with them. It is not enough to know one or even two of these points; unless we know all three, we shall be unable to arouse anger in any one. The same is true of the other emotions (Aristotle, Rhetoric 367-347 BC or 335-322 BC/1984: 91-92).

A vivid example of emotions affecting judgements is portrayed in the Norwegian expressionist painter Edvard Munch's famous picture, *The Scream*. Here the whole of reality is altered into an all-encompassing emotion, and it is obvious that the emotion fundamentally altered this person's perceptions and judgments of the world. Nothing else can take precedence. The overwhelming emotion colours the perception of the external world; the internal emotional world is so powerful that it dominates the external world too, and nothing else can penetrate the emotional experience of this depicted moment at its height. It certainly affects the person's judgment; it is certainly attended by pain. There is no explicit storyline, however: we neither know why the emotion is experienced nor what kinds of experiences, actions and judgments it may lead to.

"The Scream" by Edward Munch. 1893. (c) Stichting Beeldrecht.[1]

Munch was a devoted painter and disinterested as such in the formal features of a definition of emotions. Aristotle, on the other hand, took such philosophical matters to heart, contending that emotions are suffused with cognition. He claimed that both cause and effect are joined as necessary conditions in the definition of emotions and that these causes and effects consist of cognition or judgment, among other features.

Apparently, this Aristotelian position has been largely ignored for the past 2500 years. Emotions and reason have mainly been construed as independent spheres of influence where emotions appear as disruptive and destructive forces that rational thoughts should

---

[1] The original painting is not in black and white but in colour.

control and transform, wherein the control of unruly emotions through rationality was not regarded as incongruous (Zajonc 2000). The distinction between the various powers of the mind, including this binary classification between cognition and emotion, was preserved through the 18th and 19th centuries (Fortenbaugh 1975), continuing into contemporary times and represented in the philosopher Jerry Fodor's influential conceptualisation of the mind as modular or as having discrete modes of functioning in perception and cognition, for instance (1983).[2]

0.1 Emotions in Psychology

Psychology, as the study of human mind and behaviour, is one of the obvious scientific fields to concern itself with the nature of emotions, and its study has a fascinating past within this field. The theme of emotion and its relationship to cognition has a long history in psychology, almost as long as the science of psychology itself. Wilhelm Wundt, the founder of one of the first psychological laboratories, writes that "The clear apperception of ideas in acts of cognition and recognition is always preceded by feelings" (Wundt 1907; cited in Zajonc 1980:152). He places the domain of feelings as prior to, and independent of, conscious cognition; occurring before any thoughts or understanding have taken place. But even though emotions and their relations to cognition were studied in the early days of psychology, the nature of emotions has long been ignored in significant parts of this field. For behaviourism, a particular stimulus-response school of psychology that had its peak in the 1950's and 60's, mental life or mental properties were inappropriate, if not nonexistent, topics for scientific study. The so-called cognitive revolution of the 1970's and 1980's developed as a reaction to behaviourism and effectively ignored emotions as a topic of investigation (Eysenck and Keane 2000) with its functional conception of the mind as an analogue to the computer.

0.2 Emotions and Metaphysics

It would seem, then, that one's approach to defining and describing emotions, as well as their relationship to cognition, is largely dependent upon one's metaphysical position, i.e. the overarching

---

[2] In his later work, Fodor underscores how "modularity of mind" is only one piece of the mind puzzle (1998, 2000).

philosophical principles or theories of the constitution of the world to which one adheres. At one extreme, certain philosophers argue that there is nothing to identify because there are no such existing phenomena as mind or emotion (e.g. the analytic philosophers Daniel Dennett 1991; the Churchlands 1981; and Richard Rorty 1980/1989). To them, parlance of emotions is a contemporary instrument for coping with reality, not depicting it, and thus, emotions are merely illusions of our current use of language. Other philosophers like the Frenchman Henry-Louis Bergson, awarded the Nobel Prize for Literature in 1927 for his colourful philosophical prose, critiqued such reductionistic stances which explain the nature of experience as constituted through biological or material features alone (1888/1980). To him they are incapable of portraying deep emotions such as grief or hope. Still others consider the psycho-physical problem, or the relationship between the mind and the brain, to be the main mystery of the day; a mystery that may be solved via philosophical investigations (e.g. Thomas Nagel 2000). Conversely, it has been posited that this mind/body problem can never be solved (e.g. Colin McGinn 1989).

The study of emotions is inherently influenced by progressions in dealing with the psycho-physical problem, and one's conviction to it, either overt or covert, erects the intellectual scaffolding around one's approach to emotions and their relationship to cognition. Yet, despite these metaphysical obscurities inherent in the study of emotions, they remain amenable to scientific investigation. The various metaphysical theories and their derivations are continuously honed through scholarly critique, making some more viable than others. Nevertheless, the topic of emotions is one of the most arduous and contentious areas of study within psychology. Essentially defining and employing the term, as well as empirically investigating it, has proven exceedingly difficult, and little consensus is immediately apparent.

0.3 Emotions in "Post-modernity"
One contemporary reason for the lack of consent may be the scientific move away from modernism. One symptom of such a move is that psychology has been stretched into a vast scientific field wherein its unity is radically questioned. For instance, Steinar Kvale, a Danish psychologist, posits the impossibility of a cohesive discipline within postmodern thought, contending that the scientific base of modern

psychology shows indications of crumbling (1992). Kvale maintains his claim based upon a supposed recent cultural change from modernity to postmodernity where the underlying assumptions of modernity are being questioned; assumptions such as progression in science and technology, the existence or possibility of objective, rational discourse as well as coherent political and economic systems (McAdams 1996). Moreover, postmodernist thinkers doubt the universality of research findings and theories, and contend that what exists is not a unitary and cohesive system, but fragmented components made up of "power discourses" and "language games" (ibid.). A particular theory or movement, or any change at all, is caused by the unique circumstances of a particular spacetime with its plurality of intervening forces. Hence, an explanation is mainly valid for a particular occurrence at a particular location at a particular time, and science should focus upon "local and specific occurrences, not with the search for context-free general laws" (Polkinghore 1992:149). Postmodernity interrogates and challenges the coherence of scientific disciplines such as psychology.

The concept of postmodernity, however, is criticised for being too extreme in its claim about the disintegration of phenomena. The sociologist Anthony Giddens has named the current period as one of "high modernity" in which the current cultural change should not be viewed as the complete antithesis to modernity, but, rather, regarded as a culmination of a distinct type of social order (1990). He argues that the contemporary order consists of an increasingly disintegrated world in which there, nevertheless, exists some unity and coherence in the multitude of possibilities. An example of cohesiveness lies in the concept of postmodernity itself: postmodernity follows modernity and history is thereby given continuity (ibid.). Symptoms of the culmination of modernity have been detected in the increased tensions between theoretical psychology and clinical practice (Kvale 1992), as well as in the apparent proliferation of psychological sub-disciplines. As a manifestation of such a new era, emotion research has taken on a bewildering plurality of forms, rising from different areas of psychology. Emotions are being studied at different levels and by different methods, from research on the biological basis of emotions to investigations about the way they are being experienced, and from such divergent areas as psychoanalysis and social constructivist traditions which underscore the importance of the construed or created. According to the *Oxford Encyclopaedia of Psychology* "Psychology has witnessed a renaissance of interest in emotion in which emotion research is currently a central theme in neuroscience, development, personality, psychopathology, and culture" (2000: 162). Current discourse about emotions is directed from divergent angles through the historical prism of varying psychological schools of thought. Different studies of emotions are currently being conducted, refracting the relationship between emotion and cognition into a broad spectrum of solutions.

0.4 Emotion and Cognition

These are exciting times for thinking about emotions and their relations to cognition. There is an upsurge of interest across several sub-disciplines of psychology in emotions and their possible cognitive modulation. This book takes part in this trend and seeks to further illuminate the role of cognition in emotion. In order to do so, theories of and findings about emotion and cognition will be reviewed at three different levels of human existence: biology, functional structuring, and experience. The main focus will be an exploration of the experiential level using people's experience of the relationship between cognition and emotion. This will be done by looking at ways in which people experience visual art, because in such experiences emotion and cognition are commonly expressed. In these ways, a picture of cognition within emotion that takes into account such different conceptualizations of the relationship will be arrived at: from the biological basis to the dimension of experience.

Experience with art is the chosen subject because it is an area that easily lends itself to such studies. For instance, Lev Vygotsky and Robin George Collingwood, both famous art theorists from rather different scholarly traditions, view art as communicating feelings. Such views does not appear limited to academics, as it seems to be a common perception that art contains and elicits feelings (Kjørup 2000). Moreover, Bjarne Sode Funch, a Danish psychologist researching the existential meeting with art, delineates various contemporary psychological approaches to the appreciation of art and indirectly shows how emotions and cognition are essentially manifested and differentiated in descriptions of experiences of visual art (1997). The relationship between emotions and cognition is formulated in various forms, according to various schools of psychological thought. Experiences with art, then, can be used as a means of exploring the relationship(s) between cognition and emotion. Little research, however, is directly concerned with cognition and emotion as they are experienced, and this book attempts to address this lack of research. To this end, a study was conducted into people's actual experiences with art. It is a study of the relationship between emotion and cognition as manifested in experiences with art through interviews of museum visitors at Esbjerg Museum of Art in Denmark, a contemporary art museum that is at the forefront in studies of art presentation. The goal of this book, then, is to illuminate the role of cognition in emotions through a review of theoretical issues and through an empirical investigation into people's actual experience with art.

This book can accordingly be apportioned into distinct parts, each serving to clarify the questions "Are emotions dependent upon cognition?", and "if so, in what ways?" The first chapter deals with the nature of emotions and is an attempt to arrive at a working definition while the second details an investigation into cognitive research and the nature of cognition. Chapter three deals with relationships between cognition and emotion at different levels of psychological research while Chapter four is concerned with psychological theories of experiences with art. Chapter five describes a psychological study of peoples' experiences with art and Chapter six discusses the results of this study and their implications for the role of cognition in emotion.

The questions at hand and their implications involve one of the most fundamental questions of the structure of human experience. They are complicated and extensive, and no easy answers are to be found to the content and context of any cognitive modulation of emotion. No final overview or any definitive conclusions will be attained, rather, the relative merits of cognition in emotion will be revealed through an investigation of theoretical considerations and empirical findings within this area.

0.5 Description of Emotion Terms

So far, emotions have here been spoken of in broad terms, without specification. Although controversial, some agreement appears to exist wherein "emotion" is used to describe relatively short-lived and forceful affective experiences, while "mood", in contrast, refers to long-lasting but milder experiences. The term "affect" appears as an umbrella term, including an extensive scope of phenomena, like emotions, moods and preferences. The subjective experience of affective states has often been named "feelings" (Bennett and Hacker 2003; Davidson, Scherer and Goldsmith 2003; Eysenck and Keane 2000; Plutchik 1994). These usages of the concepts will be adhered to until further refined. Ludwig Josef Wittgenstein, however, an important philosopher of the 20th century, claimed that psychologists need, first of all, to specify the terms they use. Had the concepts employed been clarified, he contends, many experimental set-ups would have been deemed unnecessary (Bem and Jong 1997). What follows is an attempt at clarifying the nature of "emotion".

Chapter 1
Describing Emotion

According to the complete *Oxford English Dictionary* (*OED)*, in a psychological classification, the term "emotion" refers to

> a mental 'feeling' or 'affection' (e.g.: of pleasure or pain, desire or aversion, surprise, hope or fear, etc.) as distinguished from cognitive or volitional states of consciousness. Also abstr. 'feeling' as distinguished from the other classes of mental phenomena *(OED, 1994 version)*.

The *OED* states in its introduction that it attempts to include, among other forms of vocabulary, both standard conventions and core technical vocabulary. This main authority of the English language, nevertheless, gives a somewhat vague and contradictory definition in which emotions are states of consciousness distinguished from cognitive and volitional states. Emotions are regarded as subjective, first-person experiences of both sensations and intentions, and are defined through references to prototypes such as "pleasure" and "pain". As will be shown in this chapter, the process of extricating emotions as phenomena fully distinct from cognition and voluntary control has proven contentious. In line with the contemporary trend toward fragmentation, the term "emotion" has become controversial and ambiguous, even more so than the description given in the *OED*. The use of this concept is not monolithic, and several meanings can be distinguished. In what follows examples of various meanings given to emotions will be presented.

1.1 Emotions as Feelings

Emotions are frequently considered synonymous with inner "feelings" and are regarded as mental phenomena with their essence being of a subjective or introspective character, in line with the *OED*. Adherents of this viewpoint regard inner affect as the necessary feature of emotions, where "emotions" refers to subjective experiences of feelings in for instance anger or jealousy. This attitude is especially prevailing in everyday usage (Goldstein 2002).

This view of emotions being synonymous with feelings has a long historical tradition within the field of psychology. Charles Darwin allegedly undertook the first scientific study of emotion, and in his evolutionary account, Darwin identified several emotions in humans as being in kinship with the behaviours of other mammals (1872/1998).[1] He distinguished various emotions based upon their behavioural expressions but regarded the physiology and expression of emotions to be only the outer representation of inner feelings (Griffiths 1998). In his famous *Principles of Psychology* William James defines emotions as feelings: "Bodily changes follow directly the perception of the exciting fact, and that our feeling of the same changes as they occur IS the emotion" (1890/1983: 743, original capitalisation). James certainly emphasises physiological aspects as initiating emotions, yet regards the feeling component as the defining one: the feeling IS the emotion (and the feeling is awareness of bodily changes).[2]

Joseph LeDoux, a scientist who investigates the neurological underpinnings of emotions, summarises the historical importance of feeling as the identity of an emotion and states that:

> Emotion researchers, whether in psychology or in brain science, have typically sought to account for what most people think of as the essence of an emotion, the subjective experience that occurs during an emotional state- the feeling of fear when in danger, or anger when mad, or of joy when something good happens. This was clearly the goal of emotional brain theories from James through the limbic system concept (LeDoux 2002: 201).

The American analytic philosopher Saul Kripke identifies feelings as essential to mental concepts, and in his seminal philosophical paper he posits conscious mental states as designated by their qualia: the phenomenal raw feel of experience (1982). He argues that with conscious mental states it is impossible to distinguish between "how they appear" and "how they really are". The two statements are identical: their appearance, that is, their feel, is their essence - their necessary identity. Avoiding the discussion of unconscious emotions, it is here sufficient to note that many emotions become conscious and, thus, (conscious) emotions are identified by their qualia, if agreeing with Kripke. Reference to an emotion, then, can be fixed via the

---

[1] Some of the emotions he identified, for instance fear and anger, are today frequently regarded as universal "basic emotions".
[2] For a more extensive account of James' position, see William James (1884) *What is an emotion?* (1884), as well as Power and Dalgleish (1997: 30-33).

descriptive properties of the emotion, and the way it causally interacts with us. What determines these descriptive properties and causal connections is an emotion's most essential property - its raw feel (Kripke 1982).

These different accounts of emotions as feelings exemplify that the descriptions of emotions as feelings are not straightforward, and a plurality of accounts has thus been proposed concerning the nature of feelings. What "emotions as feelings" means and how to study such phenomena are topics of considerable contention. As we have seen, some claim them to reveal an awareness of somatic responses (e.g. James 1890/1983), or the raw feel of experience (e.g. Kripke 1982). Others view them as fully encultured phenomena (e.g. Kitayama and Markus 1994). Feelings being fully encultured are not regarded here as being opposed to physiology or as creating a sharp psychophysical distinction. Rather this view asserts that cultural aspects penetrate deeply into any framework in which feelings can be considered and into the way they are being felt as well. Based upon a pre-linguistic stance, however, basic undifferentiated feelings are fundamental, universal, human properties while emotions, to a greater extent, are culturally construed conceptions; emotions are both more labyrinthine and theory-filled (Wierzbicka 1994). Still different again, some researchers regard the existence of feelings as reductively inexplicable, or a part of the so-called "hard problem" of consciousness (e.g. Chalmers 1996).

Is it possible, then, that feeling, in one form or another, is essentially an irreducible feature of emotion? As will be demonstrated later, certain researchers disregard feelings as a necessary component of emotion. Moreover, there are numerous problems with feeling-based accounts of emotions, and expositions can be found in, for instance, DeSousa (1987), Plutchik (1994), Goldstein (2002) and Ben Ze've (2002). Although not an exhaustive list, the divergences in these accounts of feelings substantiate a claim toward the nature of feelings as disparate psychological phenomena. Nevertheless, these accounts have been of paramount importance to the psychology of emotion, and it seems intuitively difficult to ignore basic, raw feel in any account of the nature of emotion.

1.2 Emotions as Cognition

It is hard to find examples in psychology of emotion defined *purely* as cognition but such cognitive accounts have been claimed paradigmatic within philosophy (Salmela 2002). Common to this paradigm is the postulation that emotions are devices for information processing. Emotions are regarded as "appraisals" which are thoughts one has about a given situation relevant to one's goals and well-being (Cornelius 1996). Once the appraisals, or the cognitive content, of the emotions have been identified, there are no further questions to ask. The nature of the emotion is given. The American ethics and politics philosopher, Martha Nussbaum is one who adheres to such an account and, briefly stated, regards emotions as judgements of value, and not necessarily containing a feeling component (2001). Salmela lists philosophers who adhere to such "strong cognitive" accounts of emotions (2002: 161). Within contemporary philosophy, then, an opposition to feeling-based accounts of emotions has appeared, and a dichotomy between feeling-based and cognitive accounts of emotions has been debated throughout the past thirty years (Levinson 1998).

After the rise of cognitive science, emotions, although long ignored, have eventually been given due attention in this area of psychology, and several approaches to emotions exist within the cognitive psychological paradigm. The common denominator in these approaches is here too that emotions are regarded as results of information processing; the cognitive aspects that mainly determine what kind of emotion is being experienced. Within this cognitive psychological view, emotions are frequently positioned within the framework of "basic emotions" wherein certain emotions are viewed both as universal and as the foundation of all other emotional experience.[3] It is the routes or antecedents to emotions which are described in these different cognitive models, and they do not attempt to portray the necessary and sufficient character of emotion. The multi-component model by Power and Dalgleish is an example of

---

[3] I do not adhere to the notion of "basic emotions" because it claims emotions as universal responses that create the basis for more complex emotions. It seems to me as though the paradigm underscores the universality of basic *expressions* of emotions while ignoring the content, meaning and context of an emotion.

such an approach (1997). It describes the cognitive antecedents to emotions and views emotions within the "basic emotion" framework.

1.3 Emotions as Brain Processes

A more recent identification of emotions has occurred within neuropsychology, expanding the dichotomy between feeling-based accounts and cognitive accounts into a tripartite division including physiology. With recent strides in technical developments and current foci on emotions within neuropsychology, "emotions" sometimes refer to the brain processes correlated with "feelings of emotions". This reference is particularly used by the researchers Joseph LeDoux and Antonio Damasio who have both been instrumental in popularising neuropsychological emotion research. To them "feelings of emotions" are the subjective experiences of internal feelings such as fear and anger (Damasio 1994, 1999, 2003; LeDoux 1998, 2002).

LeDoux concludes from his research on brain activity correlations of fear responses that emotions and emotional feelings are epi-phenomena, a side effect of brain processes:

> Emotional feelings result when we become consciously aware that an emotion system of the brain is active...Emotions evolved not as conscious feelings, linguistically differentiated or not, but as brain states and bodily responses. The brain states and bodily responses are the fundamental facts of an emotion, and the conscious feelings are the frills that have added icing to the emotional cake (1998: 302).

Moreover, he claims that "(...) emotion can be defined as the process by which the brain determines or computes the value of a stimulus. Other aspects of emotion then follow from this computation" (LeDoux, 2002: 206).

Although decontextualised, it can be deduced from the two above statements that LeDoux claims the quintessence of emotions to be brain functions that evaluate stimuli for significance. This may seem identical to a cognitive approach, but LeDoux states himself that this is not the case (2002: 209). Instead his emphasis is on brain physiology and processes of transmission on a neurological level. LeDoux deems his shift in defining emotions as brain processes a necessary move due to the difficulties in studying subjective phenomena, and he, therefore, desires to understand subjective phenomena in terms of underlying processes rather than as conscious content, claiming it to be more objective.

In accord with LeDoux, Damasio views the *prima facie* of emotions to be of a physiological nature and hypothesises that the essence of an emotion is the brain process: "An emotion-proper, such as happiness, sadness, embarrassment or sympathy, is a complex collection of chemical and neural responses forming a distinctive pattern" (Damasio 2003: 53).

Damasio distinguishes between emotions and feelings, claiming that emotions are of the body and feelings of the mind (2003). Feelings, in contrast to emotions, have a subjective, first-person component, he contends. Still he extends his focus on brain processes to also include emotional feelings: emotional feelings are perceptions of bodily responses which are reactions to stimuli mediated through lower brain centres.

To both LeDoux and Damasio, brain processes that correlate with, or perhaps generate, feelings are of paramount importance and are what they actually define emotions to be.[4] By no means, however, do all neuropsychologists define emotions as brain processes. For instance, Anders Gade, a Danish neuropsychologist, briefly stated, claims that emotions consist of physiological arousal, motoric activity and subjective experience. He identifies the three components as central to most theories of emotions (1997: 339-397).

1.4 Feelings, Cognition or Brain Processes?
To conclude, there are currently at least three distinct ways of defining emotions: as feelings, as cognition and as brain processes. As shown, different branches of psychology do not just emphasise different aspects and antecedents of emotions, but claim emotions to be of a vastly different kind.[5] None of the accounts, however, bestows satisfactory explanations of emotions alone. For instance, many scientists are sceptical about studying inner aspects of mental life, and it is the publicly discernible criteria – physiological and cognitive processes that correlate with emotion – that, to them, lend credence to the understanding emotional phenomena. However, current

---

[4] For extensive critiques of LeDoux and Damasio's position on emotion, see Bennett & Hacker (2003).
[5] This line of inquiry was inspired by Funch's delineation of different kinds of art appreciation derived from different schools of psychological thought (1997).

neurophysiological and cognitive accounts cannot sufficiently distinguish between complex emotions such as shame and embarrassment, and, as will be discussed later, any such account may be deemed insufficient in explaining emotional phenomena.

If one investigates the definitions, approaches and general theories in the study of emotions, one encounters an enormous number. The examples given above are by no means meant as an exhaustive list; there are numerous ways of classifying and identifying emotions not captured in the above examples. Emotion theories differ along many dimensions. They may be distinguished in terms of their answers to the conceptual question, "What makes something an emotion?" as well as methodological and other empirical considerations which are necessarily placed within the researcher's implicit or explicit theory of what the mind is. Klaus Scherer, a prominent psychologist of the Geneva Emotion Research Group, gives an overview of different ways of viewing emotions, from dimension models to discrete models, meaning-oriented models to component models, concluding that they all have relative merits and faults, but, taken together, give the current scientific picture of what emotions are (2000). Other comprehensive overviews from the field of psychology, including historical perspectives, can be found in, for instance, Strongman's *The Psychology of Emotion* wherein over a hundred distinct, but related theories of emotions are presented (2003). See also Cornelius' *The Science of Emotion* (1996), Plutchik's *The Psychology and Biology of Emotion* (1994), as well as the anthology *Emotions: Current Issues and Future Directions,* edited by Mayne and Bonanno (2001).

1.5 Problems of Concepts and Definitions
Through the examples of definitions of emotions mentioned above, it appears as though the term "emotion" refers to different things in different fields of study, and it seems questionable as to whether emotions form a homogeneous or coherent psychological category. From such considerations several questions arise: for instance, does the variance and lack of unity with regard to the definitions imply that emotions are a varied and heterogeneous lot? Are emotions distinct phenomena consisting of heterogeneous disjointed properties? Moreover, is no single definition capable of serving as a universal, sufficient and necessary condition of emotions?

These definitions and theories cannot all be legitimate. Is there one, though, metaphysically speaking, that is correct and which distinguishes accurately between emotions and non-emotions? According to the analytic philosopher Jaegwon Kim the most accurate and complete scientific psychology is "the best overall theory about causal/nomological relations that involve mental events and states" (1996:108), i.e. the theory which most accurately can describe internal relations between mental states. Differently, Scherer asserts that the ultimate criterion for a psychological theory of emotion is its degree of compatibility with adjoining disciplines, measured through its ease, or lack thereof, in facilitating for transfer of concepts and empirical findings (2000:156). How to evaluate or test for the best psychological theory, however, resembles the wide-ranging and far-reaching debates between different branches of psychology, i.e. debates about underlying assumptions and methodology. Nevertheless, consensus seems to appear that the correct psychological theory must, additionally, give both ample behavioural and physical depictions (Kim 1996: 113). Moreover, it is generally accepted that the best psychological theory is the one with the most predictive and explanatory value.

Questions arise as to the nature of an "emotion" definition. For instance, should a definition encapsulate what experts mean by the term "emotion" or should it clarify what emotions are in common-sense psychology? Aaron Ben-Ze'ev, a philosopher of emotions, argues that a scientific definition of emotion needs a higher degree of precision than any folk-psychology, or "everyday" ways, of talking about and understanding emotions (2002). Nevertheless, it is the common folk-psychological inheritance of beliefs, desires and actions that facilitates both empathy and understanding of ancient literary actions and emotions as well as for comprehension, within limits, of many cultures throughout time that shared the same underlying principles as our contemporary folk psychology. The broad claims of folk psychology seem to be what give it great stability and generality, beyond the changing character of scientific psychology. As such, the basis for the phenomenon of folk-psychology needs elucidation, and scientific psychology attempts accurate and complete explanations of the rough phenomena of folk-psychology (Kim 1996: 108).

The German logician Gottlob Frege argues that a given concept is characterised by the attributes that define it; there exist attributes that are necessary and sufficient for giving a concept its identity (1952; cited in Eysenck and Keane 2000). Such so-called descriptive definitions, or real definitions, specify the real and essential nature of a concept – the necessary and sufficient conditions for the object's existence. Other kinds of definitions have been delineated: nominal definitions, for instance, describe the meaning of linguistic expressions without reference to "objective reality", while context or implicit definitions claim that the context in which the meaning of a term occurs specifies the term by reference to "the meaning of larger expressions" (Antonelli 1998). Normative definitions are descriptions of how one chooses to use a certain expression or term (Kjørup 2000).

As shown above, attempts have been made to give descriptive definitions of the term "emotion". Such definitions of "emotion" are suffused with incongruities, and Kjørup's argument for the impossibility of a descriptive definition of certain phenomena will be adjusted in order to make the claim that it is unfeasible to give a definitive descriptive definition of emotions (ibid.). In the psychology and philosophy of language it is a frequently held attitude that one categorises according to similarities with prototypes – a kind of standard example. Wittgenstein has given a convincing argument for language as being public events from which concepts are identified through familial resemblances (1953). These similarities are not based upon one common trait that they all share, but, rather, consist of networks of similarities within and between different elements, or subgroups, of the main category. Moreover, there are some obvious examples of the elements within the group from which comparisons are made. Accordingly, the term "emotion" cannot be given a clear definition in lay language. Nevertheless, there are some clear-cut examples of what emotions are and what they are not. It is commonly accepted that fear, anger and jealousy, for example, are emotions (Ben-Ze'ev 2000), while calculating, swimming and the startle reflex (such as an immediate reflex to alarming stimuli) are not regarded as such. It is arguable whether surprise, loneliness and different kinds of art appreciation are emotions (Ben-Ze'ev 2000: 5). Thus, the essence of emotion(s) cannot be encapsulated into a descriptive definition, which grants the necessary and sufficient characteristics of an emotion. Emotions do not have a unitary essence. They are bound together through networks of familial resemblances based upon certain prototypes. Emotions can consequently only be regarded as part of a social system, a characteristic trait being that one cannot define any one element without describing its place within the whole. It is impossible, then, to give a descriptive definition of what is an emotion and use this definition to accurately distinguish between emotions and non-emotions.

This prototype position of concept-formation may explain the phenomena of differing degrees of typicality of emotions as well as the presence of fuzzy boundaries in the distinction between emotions and non-emotions. Such a view, however, cannot adequately account for cohesiveness of categories: "(W)hat makes us group certain objects together in one category rather than in another" (Eysenck and Keane 2000: 291). In other words, the prototype position cannot explain what makes people classify something as an emotion instead of as a mood. Although there are other theories of categorisation, including the exemplar- and explanation-based views, and variations within the prototype view of characterisation[6], the example of the prototype view is sufficient for a refutation of emotions as given through a descriptive definition. Due to the complexities of emotions, it seems intuitively appealing that no such depiction can be drawn.

The refutation of a descriptive definition of emotions does not mean that we cannot achieve a closer understanding of what emotions are through attempts to identify, differentiate, describe and theorise about them. Even if one cannot refer to descriptive definitions of emotions, one can attempt to describe the role of emotions within the context and culture in which they occur, as well as their functional and physiological characteristics. Moreover, anyone can choose to give a normative definition of emotions toward their own end. Due to the variance in definition, it is no longer sufficient to imply what is meant by "emotion", but, rather, what phenomenon one refers to should be made explicitly clear.

1.6 Characteristics of Emotion

No theory or descriptive definition of emotions, then, demands common allegiance, but agreement seems to exist regarding certain characteristics of emotions. Panksepp claims it is widely acknowledged that "emotional processes have many attributes

---

[6] See Eysenck and Keane for examples (2000).

including motor-expressive, sensory-perceptual, autonomic-hormonal, cognitive-attentional, and affective-feeling aspects" (2003: 4). Along similar lines, Ben-Ze'ev argues that the prototype of an emotional experience contains several components, some more essential than others (2000, 2002). These components are: perception, feeling, imagination, memory, thought, beliefs, desires and readiness to act. At a different place in the text he states these components as cognition (meaning identification), evaluation, motivation, and feeling.[7] Moreover, Ben-Ze'ev argues that emotions are distinguished from feelings and that emotions are a "general mode", a part of a larger mental system consisting of different modalities, including the "perceptual mode" and the "intellectual mode" (ibid.). Being in an emotional mode, he argues, does not necessitate or satisfy conditions for the experience of a feeling, defined as a "simple sensation", "the lowest level of consciousness". A feeling here, thus, expresses but does not describe a subject's state of mind.

In his latest book, *Emotions revealed*, Paul Ekman, a pioneer of contemporary universal emotion studies, claims that emotions have the following characteristics:

- There is a feeling, a set of sensations, that we experience and often are aware of
- An emotional episode can be brief, sometimes lasting only a few seconds, sometimes much longer. If it lasts for hours, then it is a mood and not an emotion
- It is about something that matters to the person
- We experience emotions as happening to us, not chosen by us.
- The appraisal process, in which we are constantly scanning our environment for those things that matter to us, is usually automatic. We are not conscious of our appraising, except when it is extended over time.
- There is a refractory period that initially filters information and knowledge stored in memory, giving us access only to what supports the emotion we are feeling. The refractory period may last only a few seconds, or it may endure for much longer.
- We become aware of being emotional once the emotion has begun, when the initial appraisal is complete. Once we become conscious that we are in the grip of an emotion, we can appraise the situation.

---

[7] According to Adamos (2002: 184), Ben-Ze'ev claims that these components conglomerate into an emotion by accompanying each other, and are not connected in any causal way.

- There are universal emotional themes that reflect our evolutionary history, in addition to many culturally-learned variations that reflect our individual experience. In other words, we become emotional about matters that were relevant to our ancestors as well as ones we have found to matter in our own lives.
- The desire to experience or not experience an emotion motivates much of our behaviour.
- An affective signal – clear, rapid and universal – informs others of how the emotional person is feeling (2003: 216-217).

Guilt, shame, embarrassment and envy are exempted from having an affective signal, yet are considered emotions. In other words, they do not seem to have clear affective signals that facilitate differentiation, but are still considered to be prototypes of emotion (ibid.)

Ekman lists characteristics of emotions created as a result of empirical attempts to investigate basic universal emotions. He identifies the emotion through the causal connections of emotions, manifested in (amongst other features) regularities of facial expressions correlating with feelings in one culture. The meanings of these expressions are then investigated in other cultures. Inherent in such a cross-cultural account is a cultural partiality, and, for such universal claims to be well-founded, they should be based upon comparisons of indigenous psychologies which grow out of their own cultures (see e.g. Greenfield, 2000, for an exposition).

In the concluding chapter of the book *Emotion and Culture*, Kitayama and Markus eloquently characterise emotions (1994: 339). From their viewpoint of cultural psychology, they regard emotions as an assemblage of collectively-pooled scripts or norms, consisting of physically-, subjectively- and behaviourally-diverse component processes that are cultivated through the individual's assimilation and accommodation to their linguistic as well as other cultural practices and artefacts. Although the use of the notion "script" seems to highlight a cognitive approach, it is emphasised that culture is not about mere cognition, but also an embodiment of cultural practices, consisting of many non-cognitive components (ibid).

The question "What do all instances of emotions have in common by virtue of which they are all emotions?" can now be given a tentative answer. Through the above accounts from differing fields of psychology general characteristics of emotions can be deduced: emotions are not just feelings, or cognition, or physiology, but complex assemblages of these components, heavily influenced by the socio-cultural (including linguistic) environments in which they occur. Emotions frequently lead to a desire to act, both in order to change the current emotion as well as to communicate one's current emotional state to the surroundings. It appears dubious that all components are always present, and at the moment it appears untenable to describe any necessary or sufficient feature of emotions. Yet these features emerge in various ways, lending various emotions their differing characteristics. However, through such cluster-characterisation of emotions, one may obtain both a working characterisation from which further research can follow as well as a depiction of emotional phenomena from which distinctions between emotions and non-emotions can occur. Other affective phenomena can also be differentiated from emotions, although there will be grey areas where no unambiguous answer can be given.

This answer to the nature of emotions has consequences for debates linked to the nature of emotions. For instance, from such a list of characteristics it follows that emotions are partly subliminal, beyond awareness. Since the conscious feeling component, or any other conscious component, is frequently not considered the sole determinant of an emotion, and since several of the components occur as automatic, involuntary responses, emotional phenomena may be considered partially subliminal.

1.7 Lasting Issues?

If one accepts the assumption that emotions always, or frequently, contain a feeling component, then there are reasons why any reductive account of emotions will never fully be able to explain emotional phenomena. Chalmers argues ardently for why no evolutionary, physiological, functional (cognitive) or cultural account will be able to completely elucidate a phenomenon containing feelings (or qualia) (1996). He tries to show that an explanatory gap will arise for any reductive account of any phenomenon containing qualia as one will not be able to explain why the phenomenon under question is accompanied by subjective experience. As phrased by Ned Block, the explanatory gap "... is the idea that nothing now known about the brain, nor anything anyone has been able to imagine finding out would explain qualia" (1994). The problem of accounting for qualia is what Chalmers names "the hard problem of consciousness". The explanatory gap, so named by Levine, thus consists in the currently insufficiently explained qualia (1983). The arguments for the explanatory gap seem intuitively compelling, but as with any philosophical position, numerous counter-positions have been proposed. Several philosophers do not believe the gap exists (e.g. Rorty (1980/1989), the Churchlands (1981), Dennett (1991)). Others again (e.g. Crane 2001) does not think the explanatory gap necessarily poses a problem for reductive accounts. For instance, Crane argues that physicalism must only be committed to the causal completeness of physics, but does not need to be committed to the explanatory completeness of it. Accordingly, physicalism does not need to account for the explanatory gap, he claims. Levine, however, argues that

> A reduction should explain what is reduced, and the way we can tell whether this has been accomplished is to see whether the phenomenon to be reduced is epistemically necessitated by the reducing phenomenon (1993: 548).

Moreover, for those who believe in the existence and relevance of the explanatory gap, there are two main positions to take towards it: the so-called "inflationary" and "deflationary" positions. Some assert the gap to be closable, others do not. Holding his position, Chalmers points out that there will always be a further question to ask. Any scientific theory will be cast either in function or in structure, and even if we one day, through functional or physical description, can explain the functional role of qualia (e.g., Damasio's somatic marker hypothesis), qualia will never be vindicated, as the necessity of them would remain unexplained.

As this is no philosophical treatise, it is sufficient to conclude that there are major philosophical issues and much current debate around qualia, and that any phenomenon containing qualia may be deemed inexplicable for any reductive account of mental phenomena. Consequently, for the phenomena of emotions, there is thus the possibility that no explanatory paradigm will ever be able to fully account for their existence.

Chapter 2
Describing Cognition

The nature of emotions is somewhat opaque and attempts at clarification have yielded divergent resolutions. As was shown in the previous chapter, emotions are not simple phenomena, but, rather, appear to consist of various complex, causally related conglomerations. To describe what cognition is poses similar difficulty. Cognitive psychologists work according to different suppositions and explore a variety of phenomena. "Cognition" is a broad term, and its demarcation lines, as for the term "emotion", are hard to delineate. Despite such challenges, an attempt will be made in this chapter to illuminate the nature of cognition. Such clarification will be conducted in conjunction with enquiries into emotional phenomena and their alleged cognitive modulations.

2.1 About Cognition

"Cognition" has often been used to refer to conscious activities such as problem solving, thinking and reasoning (Eysenck and Keane 2000), wherein these events frequently have been cast as mental processes. According to the complete *Oxford English Dictionary* "cognition" is defined as

> The action or faculty of knowing; knowledge, consciousness; acquaintance with a subject; the action or faculty of knowing taken in its widest sense, including sensation, perception, conception, etc., as distinguished from feeling and volition; also, more specifically, the action of cognizing an object in perception proper (*OED*, 1994 version).

Similar to its conception of emotion, this authority of the English language describes cognition as distinct from emotion and voluntary control. Moreover, the *OED* equates cognition with consciousness as well as with knowledge. The *OED* definition, then, distinguishes emotion and volition from "knowing" processes or concepts. It will be shown in this chapter that these distinctions are in dispute. Current research from various perspectives investigates emotional and volitional processes involved in differing kinds of cognition.

The nature of cognition can be investigated through various modes of knowledge acquisition; the account of cognition is, of course, dependent upon the metaphysical theory of mind in question. Hilary Putnam, a well-known American philosopher of mind and language, proposes that mental states are computational states (1967/1975). Along these lines cognitive psychology tends to explain cognition functionally. According to Howard Gardner a primary tenet of cognitive science is that cognition is studied as "mental representations" (1985: 6), independent of both its cultural context and biological underpinning, for instance. Other central principles of cognitive psychology have also been put forward, e.g.: mental activities are regarded as information-processing modules, wherein thought and conduct are largely dependent upon mental computation and comprehension via intricate interchanges between several processes (Eysenck and Keane 2000; Griffiths 1998). These descriptions of cognition are rather abstract, but appear to give cognitive psychology an appearance of unity that is based upon certain essential assumptions. According to these, cognition, at a minimum, comprises an assortment of different kinds of information processing. Moreover, given the assumption that the field of cognitive psychology studies various representations of cognition, it becomes apparent that the term "cognition" covers a wide variety of phenomena. From Eysenck and Keane's book, *Cognitive Psychology,* it is clear that cognitive psychology, at minimum, covers visual perception; attention; memory; knowledge representation and proposition; problem solving, insight and expertise; reasoning, deduction, judgement and decision-making; language comprehension and production; creativity and discovery; as well as emotion (2000). "Cognition", then, is a broad, rather unspecified term, that encompasses at least the internal processing of different phenomena.

2.2 The Zajonc-Lazarus Debate
A debate which has aided the scientific understanding of cognition and the role of cognition in emotion took place between the researchers Robert Zajonc of Stanford University and Richard Lazarus of The University of California at Berkeley. Zajonc's article in the journal *American Psychologist* is frequently cited as the starting point of the dispute (1980). Here he asserts that affect can occur independent of, as well as prior to, cognition. Lazarus rebutted,

positing that cognition is always a part of emotion, a seemingly incompatible response (e.g. 1982, 1984, 1991 and 1999).[1] This debate over the relative importance of cognition in affect and emotion has been going on for twenty years now – intensely at times. It culminated in self-proclaimed "final statements" from both researchers as we entered the new millennium.

2.2.1 "Preferences Need No Inferences"

Zajonc's controversial statement is based on his claim that an affective evaluation of stimuli can occur immediately after perceptual registration and, most importantly, before any cognitive processes participate in the movement toward integration (1980). The affective tone of the stimuli, which can be evaluated as "positive or negative, safe or threatening", is considered primary to cognitive processing; an initial like/dislike evaluation can occur fully without any "recognition memory" of the initialising stimuli. Subsequently, he argues that emotions are frequently subconscious, and can be the first, immediate reactions to stimuli. These reactions lack cognition; "cognition" here meaning the recognition of the object. Emotions are, therefore, processed in an independent, modular system. He does not, however, claim that emotions are always independent of cognition. Certainly cognition can influence emotions, he contends, but such modulation occurs after the initial affective processing of stimuli (Zajonc e.g. 1980, 1984 and 2000)

In his 1980 paper, Zajonc clarifies what he means by the term affect and gives a nominal definition, a definition that attempts to impart linguistic meaning as described in Chapter one. Affect is an initial preference for an object; a "like-dislike" evaluation, he claims. Referring to what he regards as prototypes, he gives examples of affective reactions: "liking, disliking, preference, evaluation, or the experience of pleasure or displeasure" (Zajonc 1980: 151). He does not, however, limit affect to such responses, stating that he "deals with those aspects of affect and feeling that are generally involved in preferences" (Ibid.: 151). Other affects, such as "surprise, anger, guilt or shame", are left out. Thus, in these earlier papers, Zajonc defines the terms he uses. In his latest paper, however, he does not do so

---

[1] Other researchers have also contributed with arguments and reviewed the debate (see Lazarus for a listing (1999)).

explicitly. Rather, he uses affect, feeling and emotion interchangeably, all apparently referring to the same phenomena; he employs the terms affect, emotion and feelings synonymously. He adheres to the paradigm of "basic emotions", using its renown as an argument against a cognitive influence and states: "We speak of basic emotions. But are there basic cognition?" (2000: 46). He poses this query as support for the existence of the separation between affect and cognition. He attempts to clarify his position by giving examples of affective and cognitive prototypes, but does not use any of the proposed, basic emotions as such. Rather, he claims that "…[T]he prototype for an affective response is the individual's expressed or inferred *preference* for one stimuli over another or others" (2000: 32, original italicisation). Similarly, he contends that "the prototype of a cognitive response is the evidence of recognition of a given stimulus as familiar and thus confirming its retrieval from memory" (2000: 32). Affect is, then, indirectly equated with preference and cognition with stimulus recognition. Claiming these as affective and cognitive prototypes, respectively, is certainly controversial, and lacks precedence. Moreover, such clarification is not sufficient to establish any kind of nominal definition, although it is clearer to what phenomena he refers. As shown in the previous chapter, due to the controversies in distinguishing between affective phenomena, such an intertwined usage without differentiation or clarification is problematic.

Zajonc gives experimental evidence to support his famous statement that "preference needs no inference" (2000). He deals with the phenomenon of liking and shows that liking, or preference, for stimuli upon repeated exposure can occur without conscious recognition of stimuli. It is not a constant phenomenon, but does occur more frequently than not in experimental settings (see Bornstein for a review of the evidence (1989)). Utilising this now relatively established "mere exposure effect", Zajonc points to evidence showing that the mere exposure effect also takes place more often than not when simple stimuli are presented subliminally (2000). Changes in preference for an object can occur without awareness of the stimuli which aided the change; stimuli presented subliminally can affect the person's "preference for the stimuli previously exposed". Additionally, Zajonc has shown that participants' moods tend to improve when they view the same stimuli several times (Monahan, Murphy & Zajonc 1999; cited in Zajonc 2000).

Subsequently, there are certain main kinds of evidence that Zajonc uses to support his statement of emotion and cognition as independent, heterogeneous systems, i.e.: that emotions occur as reflexes, not under conscious control. Evidence for such a view appears along several routes.[2]

1) His main *experimental evidence* is that preference for a stimulus can be primed, with no conscious cognitive recognition occurring – the so-called "mere exposure effect". Moreover, experimental evidence demonstrates that mood changes can occur through stimuli being presented subliminally, i.e. with no conscious report of recognising the stimuli (Zajonc 2000).

2) An *evolutionary-based argument* holds that the above account of emotions has an evolutionary basis: the notion of emotions as automatic and non-cognitive carries strong evolutionary similarities to response processes in simple organisms. Additionally, both affective processes and structures are situated in areas of the brain that exist in humans as well as in these simpler organisms (Zajonc 2000).

3) The primacy of emotions has *explanatory power* that supports the hypothesis that emotions may have an involuntary and automatic nature. This primacy supports the common notion that emotions are animalistic impulses that happen to people instead of being designed and intended by them (Zajonc 2000).

4) Certain *mental disorders* (e.g. free-floating anxiety) allegedly lend evidence for affect as being of a non-conscious nature. Zajonc writes that

> Non-conscious affect has been recognised in clinical psychology in the form of the phenomenon of free-floating anxiety. Free-floating anxiety is a state – a feeling – a mood, in which the person has no idea of the origin of the feeling. It is a sort of fear, but the person does not know what he or she is afraid of, and has no idea of how to escape it. It is diffuse and non-specific. If all unconscious affect has this quality of being diffuse, un-addressed, and undedicated, then this affect should have properties that conscious affect would not have (2000: 47).

---

[2] The first three are adapted and expanded from Griffiths, 1998.

He contends, then, that subconscious affect exists wherein antecedents or causes are outside of awareness and provides for the possibility of unconscious cognition. The subjective, first-person experience of affect – here anxiety – is still present, however.

5) Joseph LeDoux's investigations into emotional reactions in animals, showing the appearance of two different neurological pathways of the fear response in rats, demonstrated that a fear response can be processed immediately and outside of consciousness (e.g. 1998, 2002).

6) Affective reactions appear to better substantiate previous experience with stimuli than do cognitive judgments (Zajonc 2000). Experimentally, however, this has only been shown for very simple stimuli.

7) Lazarus proffered that there is an ontogenesis argument which asserts that in infants and children certain objects may have inherent meanings that are not dependent upon appraisal processes. Affective experiences may, in such cases, occur without conscious appraisal (1999).

It will be argued in the following that these arguments are not strong enough to support the notion that emotion exists prior to and independent of cognition. Zajonc's claim is, accordingly, stronger than these arguments warrant. Nevertheless, certain conclusions can be drawn. One central observation is that the process of preference or liking of stimuli can occur faster than the conscious cognitive processing (recognition) of the stimuli. A second important view is that the initial unconscious processing for preference or liking of a stimulus is very different from later conscious cognitive processing. Third, mood can change (increase in hedonic tone) with the repetition of simple stimuli (see Eysenck and Keane 2000: 491).

Questions arise from Zajonc's position, however, about the nature of cognition and whether the conscious recognition of stimuli should be regarded as the first cognitive act. As Eysenck and Keane point out, Zajonc's definition of cognition is that it is analogous to consciousness or conscious phenomena; a position that has few adherents within cognitive psychology (2000). Many researchers argue that rapid and automatic processes should be named "cognitive", because they entail low-level computations (Gazzeniga,

Richard and Mangum (2002), Eysenck and Keane (2000), Power and Dalgleish (1997)).[3] Looking at what researchers within the field of cognitive psychology investigate, cognition certainly includes subliminal processes. Zajonc has, therefore, been harshly criticised for his reference toward cognition. Subconscious cognition appears as an accepted phenomenon.

2.2.2 The Necessity of Cognition in Emotion

Lazarus argued that emotions in adults are inherently dependent upon cognition (e.g. 1982, 1984, 1991, and 1999).[4] Emotions, he contended, cannot be divorced from the context in which they occur. The context, in conjunction with individual disposition, determines the appraisal of the situation, and appraisal for personal significance is necessary for the existence of an emotion. When an appraisal has been made, an emotion of a certain kind is inevitable. Emotions, then, always occur in relation to meaning; they are responses to a situation that is appraised for its personal significance. Lazarus therefore concluded that emotion always occurs after a cognitive evaluation, and that motivation is also constantly implied in an emotion. To focus on the relative primacy of any one of these processes is to miss the essential contributions of cognition and motivation to emotion, he argued.

Lazarus claimed throughout his papers that emotions consist of a conglomeration of components: thoughts, beliefs, motives, meanings, subjective bodily experiences, and physiological states. The cognitive phenomena that he referred to are forms of evaluation or appraisal, based upon learned judgments. He distinguished between primary and secondary appraisals. Primary appraisals were separated into three distinct aspects: goal relevance, goal congruence and ego involvement. These are appraisals of motivation and refer to the impact of events upon one's values, goals and commitments. Secondary appraisals shape the nature of the emotion experienced. They are related to evaluations of blame and credit, to one's potential for coping, as well as to future expectations. Both primary and secondary appraisals can occur subconsciously (Lazarus 1991). Lazarus contended that emotion always occurs in relation to meaning, but that cognition can occur without noteworthy emotion. However,

---

[3] With reference to Marr's computational metaphor for the perceptual system (1982).

[4] He also asserted that they are dependent upon motivation.

one of Lazarus' main points in his final paper is that to investigate the relative primacy between cognition and emotion is to commit "an epistemological error". In other words, the phenomena are studied in an inappropriate or invalid manner. In contrast to the experimental mode of Zajonc, Lazarus regarded the relationship of cognition to emotion as existing in a constant flow of experience. Any direction observed would depend upon one's, often arbitrary, point of entry. Hence, "any response can also be a stimulus, but not at the same instant" (Lazarus 1999: 9). Subsequently, he claimed that emotions, cognition and motivations are always fused in nature and only theoretically separable (ibid: 3).

2.2.3 Final Outline of the Debate

Ultimately, Zajonc asserts that cognition is not necessarily involved in emotion, and implies that subliminal recognition is not cognition. Lazarus challenged this first statement, arguing that cognition is an indispensable part of emotion. The debate has often been cast as a semantic controversy (e.g. Levental and Scherer 1987; Panksepp 2003), but appears to involve fundamental questions concerning how the nature of emotion and the nature of cognition can be investigated. In this regard, Zajonc concludes that affect and cognition are "independent conceptually, anatomically and dynamically in principle", although "in everyday life they interact constantly and one seldom occurs without the other" (2000:47). These positions seem incompatible, and it is questionable whether one can coherently hold to both at the same time. Inherent in the juxtaposition of these two statements is the question of the given primacy of the phenomenal level versus the physiological and/or functional level. The debate, then, contains positions that involve differences in meta-theory, and according to Lazarus, Zajonc is a neo-positivist, while he aligned himself more closely to the constructivist position (1984). Briefly stated, neo-positivism stresses objectivity and (natural) scientific proof, while constructivism emphasises how our understanding of phenomena is historically, linguistically and locally construed.

Reviewing the debate, with these last words of these two scholars in mind, it would seem as though they have been discussing dissimilar phenomena. Several times it has been pointed out that much of the debate has been based upon their differing conceptualisations of cognition. Less recognised is the likely reality that the affective phenomena in question are of different kinds. It seems uncertain whether the preference decision that Zajonc refers to can be classified as a kind of affect, as such a like/dislike statement is of a very different nature than many other affective phenomena. Currently, the criteria for inclusion and exclusion of phenomena in the affective category are unclear. Additionally, unconscious cognition appears as a robust phenomenon and is frequently involved in affective phenomena, and, arguably, always in emotional ones. Zajonc's position, therefore, appears as the more unlikely one.

2.3 Damasio's Somatic Marker Hypothesis

Damasio also investigates the nature of cognition, focusing upon the relationship between cognition and emotion. He focuses on the function of emotion in cognition. With his somatic marker hypothesis he proposes that emotions (here somatic states) are influential in decision-making processes, wherein bodily-based sensations, both positive and negative, automatically and immediately serve as points of reference for decision-making (e.g. 1994, 1996, and 1999). The emotional quality of the experience serves as an important guiding principle in cognitive appraisal – people rely intimately on their emotions for decision-making. Moreover, Damasio proposes that both unconscious and conscious sensations can serve as markers that influence conscious and non-conscious decisions.[5]

Damasio gives experimental evidence for his assertion. In the study of a patient with damage to large parts of the brain (the right frontal cortex as well as to the orbital and medial areas of the left frontal cortex), the patient's general cognitive skills were found to be intact save for a lack of sound decision-making in matters of daily living. The patient's emotional life was also severely subdued. From this correlation of phenomena, Damasio proposes that the difficulty in decision-making is based upon an inability in the patient to weigh different alternatives according to their emotional significance (Damasio 1994: 34-41). Later clinical studies by Damasio have supported the conclusions drawn from the above case-study. Patients with damage to a specific brain area (the ventral medial area of the frontal lobe) have presented with a wide variety of emotional

---

[5] Conscious sensations are unconscious ones that are given attention (Damasio 1994).

disturbances without any apparent cognitive or intellectual deficits.[6] These patients do, however, have difficulties learning from mistakes in "the gambling task", a task intended to simulate learning as it occurs in an "everyday" setting. This deficiency in learning is accompanied by an almost complete lack of anticipatory Skin Conductance Response (SCR), a measurement of the electrical conductivity of the skin. Bechara, Damasio and Damasio posit that healthy subjects acquire an anticipatory SCR as an emotional reaction to the potential consequences of their actions (1999). The anticipatory SCR is a measurable manifestation of the somatic marker, they claim. Accordingly, the patients lack the somatic marker that would aid them in proper decision-making.

Damasio's experiential evidence does not appear robust. The assertion that the SCR is a constant phenomenon in healthy subjects seems debatable since several of the healthy subjects did not develop it according to expectations (see Bechara, Damasio and Damasio 1999). Few studies seem be able to duplicate these results and a review article of the somatic marker hypothesis by Dunn, Dalgleish and Lawrence in 2006 concludes that it lacks empirical support.

2.4 Embodied Cognition

Damasio emphasises that somatic experiences play a role in cognition. A long-lasting, prevailing attitude within cognitive psychology, however, has been the notion of thought as abstract, logical processes, independent of the body (Lakoff and Johnson 1999). Through contemporary research it has become clear that the body influences cognitive processes. "The body", however, can refer to both bodily experiences in the phenomenological capacity as well as to sensory-motoric processes (Shanon 1993). In Merleau-Ponty's *Phenomenology of perception* the body is viewed as the starting point for subjectivity (1945). From his thesis, a new line of thought develops where the body forms the core for understanding. The body is primary, determining what we can know and how we can know it. The role of the body in thought has been subsequently investigated by, for instance, Johnson (1987) and Lakoff and Johnson (1999). They underscore the bodily basis of conceptualisation and meaning-creation, showing how our bodily-based experiences shape language,

---

[6] Established in for instance Wisconsin Card Sorting Task and Tower of London (Turnbull et al. 2003).

particularly the use of metaphors. Metaphors are not products of random selections. They arise from certain correlations in our experience, wherein concepts become associated with other concepts partly because of our bodily-based experience of them. Lakoff gives the example of anger and shows how characteristic forms of anger language have complex and varied cognitive configurations (1987). These cognitive structures that demarcate anger are based, in part, upon the bodily manifestation of experience. For instance, the common metaphor "anger is heat", arose out of the physiological changes of increased corporal heat that frequently correlates with the subjective experience of anger. The general metaphor "anger is heat" can be found in many English expressions from "you make my blood boil", to "simmer down", "I had reached the boiling point" and "they were having a heated argument" (examples given by Lakoff 1987: 382-383). These examples underscore that the way one speaks about anger is based upon bodily experiences of anger, and that from such experiences, complex cognitive, linguistic structures for anger arise (see e.g. Johnson 1987; Lakoff 1987 and Kövecses 2000, for other examples).The "basic-level category structure" of anger is grounded in the sensory-motoric nature of human encounters. From sensory-motoric experiences, the mode in which one speaks about anger obtains an intricate conceptual (cognitive) content. Our bodily-based experiences structure, at least partly, the way we think; our conceptual system is dependent upon interactions between our bodies and their environments.

2.5 Concluding Remarks
Currently, "cognition" refers to a wide variety of phenomena that can be investigated relatively independently. Cognitive psychologists explore and model fundamental processes, such as registration and encoding, which are involved in various forms of cognition. Cognitive psychology appears to investigate and model different cognitive processes in accord with certain essential tenets. The studies of cognition, then, seem rather different from investigations of emotion. The use of the term "cognition", however, appears similar to "emotion" as a broad and general expression that encompasses various constituent features and events.

From the Zajonc-Lazarus debate, it is evident that preference decisions can be made without conscious recognition of stimuli. Also, unconscious cognition appears as a robust phenomenon with its nature(s) yet to be determined. Lazarus underscores how cognition, motivation and emotion appear in one confluent stream of experience, and that any separation of the phenomena is artificial. Motivation and cognition are always a part of an emotion, he contends. Damasio stresses that sensations are profoundly involved in cognition. Sensations (to Damasio, emotions) are necessary for effective reasoning and he highlights the function of bodily-based sensations in the process of assigning values to alternatives. Empirical studies have not yielded uniform results in regard to the somatic marker hypothesis. It is, nevertheless, a theoretical possibility, and the role of emotion in cognition is currently a relatively hot topic for scientific studies (see, for instance, Forgas 2003; Loewenstein and Lerner 2003).

The traditions that investigate embodied cognition highlight that thoughts are directly dependent upon the body, both in a phenomenological sense as well as in the more pragmatic sense of direct somatic experience. From these traditions one can conclude that the various cognitive phenomena are not independent and abstract processes, but at least partly originate from bodily experience. The distinction between cognition and emotion no longer involves a completely dualist account, as thoughts are also entrenched in the body. Within the latter tradition, at least, cognition is a broad concept that is used to include affective phenomena. It is shown that the way emotions are conceptualised and understood is partly dependent upon these kinds of cognition.

What follows is a brief description of the postulated modulation of cognition in emotion, as manifested in various theories at different levels of concern. Through such description, one can arrive at a demarcation of the status of cognition in emotion in contemporary research, thereby emphasising the differences and similarities in conceptualisation and results across the various manners of research.

Chapter 3
Theories about the Emotion-Cognition Relationship

There are many thorny dilemmas inherent in the clarification of the role of cognition in emotions. A pertinent one is its level of clarification. Phenomenologists like Edmund Husserl and Maurice Merleau-Ponty argue that "truth about human existence" has to be founded on the phenomenal level, that is, at the level of experience. The prominent linguists Noam Chomsky and Jerry Fodor insist on a functionalist priority: explaining a mental phenomenon by way of its function in relation to other mental states. Eliminativists would, by definition, grant explanatory and defining power to the neural level (Lakoff and Johnson 1999). Lakoff and Johnson (ibid: 109) themselves argue that "There is no unique correct description of any situation" (ibid: 109). They contend that since the embodiment of the human psyche occurs throughout several strata no one stratum can elucidate all truths. Different levels will explain a variety of phenomena for diverse purposes. Similar thoughts are not foreign to the art world either, and Joseph Kosuth, the American concept artist, has depicted different levels of presentation. In his installation piece, *One and Three Chairs* (1965), a chair, a picture of a chair and a picture of the definition of a chair given in a dictionary are presented, thereby opening up for concrete experiences of various levels of representation.

In this chapter there will be no presentation of the relationship between cognition and emotion which claims any artistic merit. Instead examples of psychological theories will be given concerning the relationship between emotion and cognition at the three major levels of theoretical concern.

3.1 The Neuropsychological Level
Within the field of neuropsychology, the alleged dichotomy between cognition and thinking has been feverishly debated and remains, after twenty-five years of research, a contentious topic. LeDoux (see Chapter one) is one of the prominent researchers who has coloured the debate and has allegedly given evidence for emotion and cognition as being distinct phenomena. One of his crucial points has been whether

emotion and cognition are processed through independent brain routes. LeDoux argues for a separation between cognitive and emotional processing, and appears to obtain his evidence from two main sources: studies of fear conditioning in rats and studies of a particular kind of brain damage in humans.

3.1.1 Conditioning of Fear in Rats

LeDoux shows that fear reactions can be processed through two different brain routes in rats: one cortical and one sub-cortical (e.g. 1996, 1998). The subcortical route is much faster than the cortical, and is advantageous for, among other things, the processing of warning signals. The cortical route involves processing that goes from the brain structures of the thalamus, through the cortex and then to amygdala whereas the sub-cortical route goes directly from the thalamus to amygdala. LeDoux proposes that fear reactions are processed similarly in humans; affectively elicited actions can, in certain cases, take place before the conscious mind has time to intervene, but at other times consciousness is involved. Stimuli eliciting emotions can be processed both with and without conscious cognition, he contends. It is, for ethical reasons, currently difficult to establish the existence of such pathways in humans although it is being investigated with new brain imaging techniques. These studies are in their beginning phases and their results appear, so far, inconclusive (see, e.g. Phan et al. 2002 who have conducted a meta-analysis of such studies).

3.1.2 Split-Brain Patients

From his early studies on split-brain patients – patients who had had the main connection between the two different brain hemispheres severed – LeDoux reached the conclusion that "Split brain surgery seemed to be revealing a fundamental psychological dichotomy between thinking and feeling, between cognition and emotion" (1998: 15). He based his claim on the discovery of a patient for whom emotional stimuli and cognitive stimuli allegedly bifurcated into distinct routes of information processing, meaning that emotional and cognitive information seemed to be processed through different neuronal pathways in the brain. For the patient in question, the main pathway, the corpus callosum was partitioned, while the other pathway, the anterior commisure, remained intact. Following the sectioning, the patient was not able to verbally report the identity of stimuli presented to his right hemisphere, but only when they were presented to his left. In regards to the emotional content of the stimuli, the facts were different. When emotional stimuli were delivered to the right hemisphere, the patient was able to give some emotional information about the stimuli. The patient was able to decide whether the stimuli represented something "emotionally good or bad", although not able to verbally describe it. Hence, the emotional content of the stimuli was thought to pass through a neuronal route through which the cognitive information could not. LeDoux interprets this to mean that "The right hemisphere was unable to share its thoughts about what the stimulus was with the left, but was able to transfer the emotional meaning of the stimulus over" (LeDoux 1998: 15; see also Gazzeniga et al. 2002).

The studies of this patient are described in Gazzeniga and LeDoux's book, *The Integrated Mind* (1978: 21, 85-88, 142-155). After a thorough investigation of this text, the results of these studies reveal a more complex picture, rendering LeDoux's above-mentioned results more difficult to interpret. For instance, the patient completed a verbal command test in which written action commands having emotionally provocative content were presented to the right hemisphere. The patient could verbalise some crude emotional valence statements ("good" or "bad"), and was able to follow commands. The patient could *point* to the correct identity of the object, but could not verbally state its identity. Therefore, it appears as though the dissociation is more complex that LeDoux described (1998). It is not necessarily the cognitive information which is dissociated from the emotional content as there appears to exist a separation between the verbal and otherwise behavioural functions for identification. Instead of there being different brain routes for cognitive and emotional stimuli, the case seems to involve a dichotomy in which behavioural identification can be induced when lateralised to either hemisphere, while verbal identification proves to be different. The case, therefore, appears less clear-cut than LeDoux contends (1998). Additionally, the set-up does not appear to differentiate between recognising and experiencing emotion, further confounding the case. Moreover, when completing a literature search, no other articles appear in which emotion and cognition are investigated following split brain surgery. LeDoux's statement is lacking, then, both in generalisability and in validity.

3.1.3 Separate Systems?

Jaak Panksepp, a neuropsychologist, argues that at the neuro-psychological level a clear distinction between emotion and cognition appears (2003). Moreover, he contends that it is essential to maintain this distinction for pragmatic reasons, specifically to better and faster investigate the neuropsychological bases of affect, and to continue essential and focused research that is common to both humans and lower-level organisms. He does underscore, though, how cognition and emotions are profoundly interwoven at a subjective, first-person level. In his paper, the terms affect, emotion and feeling are employed interchangeably, all apparently referring to the same phenomenon that is "an ancient form of consciousness shared by all mammals" (ibid.: 7). He puts forth several arguments to support his statements, including assertions that affects contain "the presence of experienced valence" (ibid.: 4), while cognition do not, as well as evidence that affects are sub-cortical and cognition cortical. In addition, he explains that affect and cognition show differentiations following brain damage wherein emotional responses may remain intact while cognition is thoroughly impaired. It is also shown that affect and cognition are developmentally distinct, as children are more developed affectively than cognitively, he contends. Finally, emotions are recognised as universal while cognition are not, and affects tend to be located within the right hemisphere while cognition appear to reside in the left.

Richard Davidson, also a neuropsychologist, argues against Panksepp, contending that affective and cognitive processes are deeply connected (2003). He refers to research showing that there are overlaps in the neural circuits of affects and cognition. In a co-authored book chapter on neuroimaging and human emotion, Pizzagalli, Schakman and Davidson contend that the brain area of the prefrontal cortex, for instance, is an area wherein cognition and affects are processed as intertwined (2003). Differences between emotional states might only be discovered through investigations into cognition, attention, memory and biological changes, they argue.

In line with Panksepp and LeDoux, several other neuropsychological researchers point out that affect can be directly related to a separate, primary response system. Proponents of this position weigh in on the side of evolutionary importance of emotions for decision-making, evaluation and action. An evolutionary function of emotions is to evaluate information that may lead to increased attention towards essential matters of survival. Such affective responses are developed from the beginning of life and may become ingrained in differentiated emotional systems. One thesis, then, is that the different emotional systems represent different degrees of integration between cognitive and affective structures, so that affects can be perceived as occurring without cognition and as directly dependent upon context while, at the same time, taking part in changing cognitive processes throughout the life span (Adolph and Damasio 2001). It may be, then, that Panksepp and Davison, in effect, are discussing different phenomena. Panksepp's emotions, "an ancient form of consciousness shared by all mammals" (2003: 7), appear as only representative of a small portion of emotional phenomena. Hence, it seems to be underscored how affective phenomena are a heterogeneous lot, wherein cognition is involved to a various and undetermined extent. Another main point that arises is whether the automatic, evolutionary-based responses such as immediate fear response should be considered as emotion, affect, or neither. The criteria for depicting an emotion are unclear. Moreover, reviews of the neuropsychological field in the *Handbook of affective sciences* (edited by Davidson, Scherer and Goldsmith 2003) make it clear that no consensus has been reached regarding the relationship between cognition and emotion at a neuropsychological level. The evidence for cognition and emotion as separate systems, or vice versa, is inconclusive.

3.2 The Functional Level
Several theories exist at a functional level that attempt to model or represent the functioning of the emotive/cognitive relationship. For instance, clinical theories can be said to exist at a functional level. Psychoanalysis, broadly speaking, is one such theory.

3.2.1 Psychoanalysis
Psychoanalysis can be said to have the goal of obtaining personal understanding of one's unconscious forces, frequently of an emotional nature. Extrapolating from Freud's writings (1920, 1923-25), tension between cognition and emotion may be said to lie within the pleasure

principle and the reality principle. The pleasure principle is a metaphor for the tendency of the mind to strive toward pleasure and to avoid unpleasure, pleasure and unpleasure being fundamental orienting principles for the psyche (1920/1961: 6). The search for pleasure is modified through the reality principle via the ego's sense of self conservation, in order to avoid harm to one's individual life. The reality principle holds pleasure as its aspiration, but a pleasure that is anchored in reality. The search for pleasure can then be postponed or reduced in intensity. The pleasure principle and the reality principle are universal propensities of the mind, and a proper balance between the two is decisive in how one conducts one's life. Thus, within Freudian psychoanalysis, emotion (as pleasure) can be said to be a fundamental notion that cognition, as a means of conceptualising and understanding of reality, needs to control. Freud underscores that "…[T]he ego represents what may be called reason and common sense, in contrast with the id, which contains the passions" (1923-25/1961: 25). Such suppositions about the relationship between emotion and cognition are closely linked to philosophical and religious traditions wherein the passions need to be controlled by reason.

3.2.2 Cognitive Label of General Arousal

The function of cognition in emotions is also investigated within several experimental paradigms. For instance, Schachter and Singer explore how emotions come into function; they examine the role of cognitive appraisal or evaluation in the making of an emotion (1962). Their famous, but faulty, experiment leads to their conclusion that emotions are a function of cognitive labels of general arousal. In the experiment some of the participants are unknowingly injected with adrenalin, believing they received vitamins. The participants are then placed in a set-up where an actor responds to a situation in a particular way. The main results are that the participant's interpreted their physiological responses in accordance with the actor; in accordance with the clues given. Based on this, Schachter and Singer conclude that "…[P]recisely the same state of physiological arousal could be labelled 'joy' or 'fury' or 'jealousy' or any of a great diversity of emotional labels depending on the cognitive aspect of the situation" (Ibid. 1962: 398). Therefore, it is the cognitive aspect which determines the kind of emotion experienced. The emotion involves a felt aspect (physiological arousal) that is given a cognitively-based label. The necessary and sufficient conditions for emotions are physiological arousal and cognition, Schachter and Singer contend. There have been great difficulties in replicating this study, however (For critiques of the experiment see e.g. Power and Dagleigh 1997).

3.2.3 Cognitive Models

Two newer examples of cognitive, or functional, models that attempt to portray the role of cognition in emotion are given by three cognitive psychologists, Power and Dagleigh (1997) and Teasdale (1999). The former approach by Power and Dagleigh is a cognitive model that attempts to build on two routes of emotional processing: one which can be processed quickly and automatically, and the other which is slower and contains more extensive cognitive processing. The automatic route is modulated by associations between biologically-based reactions and particular responses (e.g. nauseous aversion to food or fear reactions to snakes (Teasdale 1999)). For the slower, cognitive route, other representational systems may also be involved (for more detail, see Power and Dagleigh 1997, and Teasdale 1999). The latter model by Teasdale details a relationship between cognition and emotion based on clinical research (1999). It is a model that depicts cognition involved in depression. Without describing his model, it is sufficient to say that he views affects and cognition as thoroughly interconnected in the clinical phenomenon he attempts to delineate. These two cognitive models attempt to exemplify how the cognitive-affective relationships can indeed function.

3.2.4 The Problem of Experience

Research at both neuropsychological and functional levels is being conducted that illuminates the role of cognition in emotion. These theories as shown, however, are filled with controversy, and no unequivocal account seems to appear. LeDoux and Panksepp argue for a clear distinction between emotion and cognition. It seems apparent that Panksepp investigates emotions from an evolutionistic point of view and has a particular kind of emotion in mind when he arrives at his conclusions. The Panksepp-Davidson debate may prove itself solved, to some extent, if one clarifies what the phenomena in question are – it may be that they investigate dissimilar phenomena. Similarly, LeDoux has a particular kind of fear in mind when he investigates the correlations between neuronal routes involved in a fear response. As Wittgenstein observed, however, fear is not a simple phenomenon (1945/1958). It has a wide variety of meanings that can be investigated according to the context in which it occurs.

At a functional level, Schachter and Singer's experiment has been deemed invalid, and psychoanalysis has undergone riveting developments since Freud's times. The newer cognitive models[1], however, depict functional means, according to findings at both neurological and phenomenal levels. According to their, as yet unknown, levels of accuracy, these models will have a certain power to predict and explain the phenomena at hand. Their postulated relationships between emotion and cognition will, then, have a chance to be verified and adjusted. A main problem for both neurological and functional theories of mental events, however, is that they currently lack the power to explain qualitative aspects of experience. The qualitative aspects of experience such as feelings and sensations are the very topics for which neurological (physicalist) and cognitive (functionalist) theories are unable to account (Kim 1996; Chalmers 1996).

3.3 The Phenomenal Level

The relationship between emotion and cognition is also a topic for phenomenological investigation. Ken Strongman, a psychologist concerned with emotion research, argues that any full theory of emotion must be based upon, or minimally include, a phenomenological level (2003). In his words, such a theory must "(…) be grounded in everyday experience" (ibid: 297). Ernesto Spinelli, a contemporary existential psychologist, elegantly proffers that "as a science whose purported aim is the understanding of man, psychology's starting point must be the exploration of human experience" (1989: 184). He argues that phenomenological psychology is likely to become crucial for the task of reaching greater consistency and accord within psychology amidst the contemporary fragmentation within psychology. Phenomenological psychology, he contends, does not refute research from other branches of psychology, but, essentially, elucidates foregone suppositions and conclusions. It

---

[1] Along with newer clinical models not discussed here.

can also identify likely junctions between different areas of psychology where connections can fruitfully be made.

Subsequently, it appears as though several phenomena need demarcating from one another according to their existence at the phenomenal level. The affective area seems to consist of phenomena wherein such a clarification is needed. Numerous experimental results seem inaccurate because the phenomenon under investigation has not been clarified phenomenologically. Thus, research at the phenomenal level not only exists as an independent mode of inquiry, but also serves as to correct and clarify further research conducted at other levels, delineating the phenomena at hand. Without venturing into an extensive debate about the role of psychological phenomenology and its relation to psychology's "harder", more natural-scientific, parts, it is sufficient to note here that one of the functions of psychological phenomenology is to give direction and clarification to empirical research at other levels of inquiry.

Debates and investigations about relationships between cognition and emotion on a phenomenal level seem currently less frequent than at the neuropsychological and functional levels, but are of primary importance. Bjarne Sode Funch, a Danish existential psychologist, calls for phenomenological research into emotions (1997). Phenomenological research into the depiction of cognition in emotion is a step in that direction. Through such investigation, one can illuminate people's experiences of the relationship between emotion and cognition, beyond the platitudes of everyday talk, which any theory accounting for emotion as well as the relationship between cognition and emotion must coherently accommodate.

Strongman devotes a chapter to phenomenological theories of emotions (2003). The relationship between emotion and consciousness is the main topic; the connection between emotion and cognition being of secondary importance. These different phenomenologists conceptualise emotion and cognition differently, however, including varying depictions of their relationship. Here the theories of Stumpf, Sartre, Buytedjik and Hillmann will be expounded upon, because these theories represent different manners of viewing the relationship between cognition and emotion, contain different problems and lend different benefits to the task at hand. Funch's recent depiction of the cognitive-emotive relationship at a phenomenal level will also be described, which appears implicit in his investigations into the aesthetic experience (1997).

3.3.1 Early Accounts

Carl Stumpf, a German psychologist and philosopher, developed a theory of emotion (e.g. 1899; cited in Reisenzein and Schönpflug 1992). He claimed that all mental states are intentional and that there are two main mental categories: intellectual and affective (Stumpf refers to the emotions when he uses the term "affective"). These two categories are of a fundamentally different kind and have different intentional relations to objects. The affective category is further separated into active versus passive states. The active states involve varying kinds of desires and intentions while the passive states include "for and against evaluations of various states of affairs" (Strongman 2003: 23). The affective categories are all of a cognitive nature as they are based upon certain kinds of evaluations, and it is a cognitive-evaluative theory of emotions (Reisenzein and Schönpflug 1992).

Edmund Husserl is regarded as the founder of phenomenology - a branch of philosophy which concerns itself with the nature of consciousness including the modes in which phenomena appear to consciousness. Husserl contended that emotions, belief and desires are intentional: they have a particular directedness upon an object. The intentions come from the "essential person" or a transcendental ego (Sartre 1937). Sartre argued against Husserl's idea of a transcendental ego (1937). He refuted an inner essence, or ego, as a point of origin for actions, emotions and character. He contended that consciousness is created by one's self-image and by the views others have of one, arrived at through past behaviours and feelings. Consciousness does not contain an "I", but is impersonal or, at most, pre-personal. What this means is that consciousness is shaped by its intentions (Sartre 1937). We give things their meaning according to the intentions through which we view the world. To exist at all, consciousness has to have an object about which to be conscious. Also, conscious beings can never escape from acting freely in the world, because consciousness is, in essence, the same as freedom. We can choose to see things as frightening or beautiful, disgusting or attractive, and from this kind of choice springs our character, our attitudes, our emotions and our way of life. Thus, for Sartre "existence comes before essence" (Sartre 1943/1984).

Emotion, according to Sartre, is a separate mode of consciousness, and if the experience of an emotion is genuine, it is also non-reflective. In other words, it cannot take itself as an object and reflect upon itself. A genuine emotion cannot be controlled. Hence, genuine emotions are independent of conscious cognition as they are experienced. According to Sartre, an emotion is a way of comprehending the world that, at the same time, transforms it. The world perceived through an emotion is altered into having a new quality, as can seen in *The Scream* by Munch mentioned in Chapter one. Sartrean emotions, moreover, generate a fully consistent world that is amplified. These emotions lead to or are a separate mode of existence that has a transcendental quality (Strongman 2003). The origin of emotion, according to Sartre's theory, seems incomprehensible and not sufficiently answered in his theory, while Strongman contends that emotions, in Sartre's metaphysics, "originates in a spontaneous debasement lived by the consciousness in the face of the world" (ibid.: 25). According to Strongman's interpretation, then, emotions appear as spontaneous acts which, at the same time, are responses or evaluations of a situation for personal significance.

Conclusively, Sartre's views of emotions were strongly linked to his metaphysics, including his ideas about subjectivity and freedom. Sartre wrote from the position of existential phenomenology, and his investigations of emotions can be viewed as a part of his development of a metaphysics. Sartre's particular line of thought, however, has been discredited from several other philosophical traditions, such as structuralist and post-structuralist schools of thought. For instance, the famous anthropologist Claude Levi-Strauss in *La pensee sauvage* criticised Sartre severely (1962/1995). He held Sartre's existentialism as a contemporary myth. Sartre's metaphysics leads to an "illusion of freedom" and an artificial distancing of humanity from nature, he claimed.

3.3.2 Later Accounts

Frederik Buytendjik argued that feelings (emotions) are meaningful because of their signifier; feelings are responses to situations with personal significance and meaning, and have a function to confirm our system of beliefs (1950; cited in Strongman 2003). At the same time, emotions are non-intentional, spontaneous and invoke a felt aspect that determines the quality of existence. Moreover, they can be altered by cognition. In this theory, then, emotions are consequences of cognition, yet have cognitive effects. Along a similar line, James Hillmann, in a phenomenological analysis, adheres to a cognitive approach to emotions (1960). He follows Aristotle's system for causality wherein emotions include distinct causes (Strongman 2003).

A recent phenomenological account of emotions that includes relations to cognition is given by Funch (1997). He regards emotions to be determined by their "existential actuality", meaning that the quality of an emotion is a function of the existential dilemmas that elicit it. It is the awareness of the situation's existential importance that primarily determines the nature of the emotion. Funch bases the primacy of the "existential actuality" upon the "simple phenomenological fact that emotions are usually established in experience with sensation or imagination, before any bodily responses have reached the mind" (ibid.: 243). Bodily actions and reactions adjust rather than determine the experience. Emotions may lack explicit corporeal appearance as well as cognition, he contends. When cognition occurs in relation to emotions they can take the form of evaluations of the situation for existential significance or as interpretations of bodily reactions. Cognition are always secondary to sensations; sensations here referring to "sensory manifestation" or experiences of bodily reactions. The experience of an emotion is not necessarily triggered by external stimuli - as imagination can establish an emotion. There is no such thing as a finite number of basic emotions, but endless possibilities for variations. Moreover, an emotion is a part of an event, and only in exceptional cases does it constitute the complete experience.

Funch posits that the essential feel of complex emotions with high existential density seems to lack unity. Such feel is of various kinds and there are there are multiple causes. He gives the example of grief and the difficulty of giving exact characteristics and explanations of it. However, he also states that

> emotional qualities are fundamental psychological entities, and apart from their acute presence within experience they cannot be further determined or described. Only as they are linked to other aspects in their existential actuality can they become accessible for reflection and further analysis (Funch 1997: 255).

It appears, then, as if Funch differentiates between complex emotions and a more basic, or fundamental, psychological entity. It may be that what he postulates is an emotionally-coloured raw feel of experience.

3.3.3 Concluding Remarks

The above account of phenomenological theories of the relationship between cognition and emotion is a brief exposition of the cognitive-emotive relationship at a phenomenal level. Stumpf argues for a differentiation between intellective and affective (emotional) functioning, although affect contains a cognitive aspect. Sartre theorises that emotions are a separate mode of consciousness that heavily influences cognition. Buytendjik and Hillman both contend that emotions are reactions to evaluations. Funch asserts that the experience of an emotion may lack cognition. These theories externally contradict one another and focus upon different emotional aspects. To resolve these tensions, further phenomenological studies of emotions and their relation to cognition are essential. Qualitative investigations, which utilise new tools of qualitative analysis wherein concrete emotional experiences are under focus, are imperative.

What follows, then, is a qualitative study of art appreciation. Art appreciation consists of events that are rich in experience and elicit strong emotional and cognitive reactions. It has been chosen as a catalyst for indirect expressions of the relationship between emotion and cognition at a phenomenal level, meaning that through people's experiences with art, actualisations of emotion and cognition in consciousness can be examined. But before venturing into the details of the study, a review will be conducted of the literature concerning art appreciation and the implied relationship between emotion and cognition.

Chapter 4
Experiences with Art

In *The Psychology of Art Appreciation* Funch conducts an extensive investigation into how various schools of psychological thought view and study experiences with art (1997). It is probably the most comprehensive overview of the ways in which experiences with art are treated within psychology today. He shows how experiences with art have been conceptualised within various psychological traditions and, thereby, implicitly how emotion and cognition are given different relevance dependent upon how the nature of experience is viewed. Funch uses the term "art appreciation" and shows how different psychological schools of thought have viewed it. Philosophically, however, it has been difficult to assert the content of the term "art appreciation", i.e. what it actually means. It can, for instance, refer to a kind of pleasure or a particular type of judgment (Woodfield 1999). In relation to art it seems particularly difficult to assert what the opposite, "not to appreciate", means as, for instance, reactions of disgust or of anger might indeed be what is intended by the artist. Moving through more concrete and less philosophical realms, Funch tackles this issue directly and depicts four distinct forms of art appreciation based upon phenomenological considerations as well as introspective studies, empirical research, and theoretical ideation, all mainly in relation to artistic pictures. "Art appreciation" is distinguished into "aesthetic pleasure", "emotional appreciation", "cognitive art appreciation", and "aesthetic fascination". Furthermore he conceptualises a fifth form: "the aesthetic experience". Throughout his investigation, Funch shows how different schools of thought have confined themselves to certain kinds of art appreciation. Aesthetic pleasure originates from the psycho-physical tradition in which the art work elicits physiologically-based sensations which are pleasurable while cognitive traditions emphasise an intellectual approach to art appreciation. Gestalt psychology posits an emotional form of art appreciation while psychoanalysis asserts the form of art appreciation named "aesthetic fascination". Funch regards the aesthetic experience, which he develops within the existential-phenomenological school of thought, as the ultimate form of art appreciation, and investigates and describes psychological benefits of the aesthetic experience.

Through Funch's investigation into the differing ways experiences with art have been conceptualised in psychology, it is evident that distinct phenomena have been proposed as to the way in which art is experienced. The differing experiences have certain characteristics which distinguish them from each other. The following is an overview of the different categories of aesthetic pleasure, art understanding, emotional appreciation and aesthetic fascination as well as the aesthetic experience as described by Funch. Related research conducted after Funch's investigation has been incorporated into the relevant sections, and it should be clear from the context when this occurs. The point here is not to continue to argue for a certain view of what experience is, but to present an outline of views of experiences with art within different psychological traditions, although some of these modes of explanation and ways of viewing experience are more probable than others.

4.1 Aesthetic Pleasure

From the psycho-physical tradition, experiences with art arise from humans' "natural" biological constitution; researchers within this tradition emphasise our biological constitution, including the necessary neural mechanisms, as the primary factor influencing our perception and experience of art. Here the experience of art is viewed as leading to a feeling of pleasure, a form of sensory pleasure named "aesthetic pleasure". It is an instantaneous, fundamental and inherently pleasurable reaction to the art work, void of any other features save a "bodily- based" sensation. A number of visual features leading to such sensation have been proposed and investigated: certain configurations of colour harmonies, structures within paintings giving shape to the "golden section"[1], as well as unidentified features of the art work. These provoke movements of the eyes that are graceful and, therefore, pleasurable. The psycho-physical tradition endeavours to specify formal features of art works which give rise to such pleasurable sensations. Investigations have also been conducted into aesthetic sensitivity and aesthetic personality in order to question

---

[1] The golden section is a particular geometrical shape that has been investigated for its "pleasing-ness". It takes a cross-like shape, wherein the ratio between the different parts is approximately eight to five (Funch 1997: 12).

whether there exist characteristics within an individual that facilitate such experiences. These investigations have been rather inconclusive so far, but are further illuminated within the various remaining delineations of experiences with art (Funch 1997).

The sensory pleasure that arises when viewing art has been considered to be a sensation steadfastly coupled with "pure" perception processes; that is, perception cleansed of all other influencing mental activity. The cognition involved is minimal, researchers within this tradition contend. From a cognitive stance, however, it has been questioned whether such a sensation is linked to other phenomena. Maybe the sensation of pleasure is linked to certain types of cognition antecedent of the pleasurable response, and maybe the feeling of pleasure originates from the kind of cognition involved (Funch 1997). Nevertheless, within this framework for viewing aesthetic pleasure emotions are, in principle, only involved if the relatively immediate and basic sensory pleasure is regarded as an emotion.

Within the contemporary psycho-physical tradition of vision research, much attention is devoted to the perception of art objects. Ramachandran and Hirstein, two contemporary neuroscientists, attempt to identify neural mechanisms necessary for artistic experiences (1999). They propose eight heuristics that are used to stimulate visual areas of the brain. These heuristics are allegedly employed in both making and viewing art. One of the main principles they name is "the peak shift effect", a principle established in discrimination tasks in animals. For instance, if a rat learns to discriminate between geometrical forms and is rewarded for responding to a rectangle, the rat will respond more vigorously to a rectangle which has its forms exaggerated, compared to the prototype to which the rat was trained. The explanation given for this effect is that the rat has learned to identify through the help of a rule, namely rectangularity, and not by the set, accurate features or proportions of the prototype it was trained to. Based on these results, they argue that artists exaggerate the form of the prototype they are painting, and the viewer's visual areas become stimulated to an extent that would not occur if the peak shift effect was not employed. Another principle, grouping, occurs through the discovery of relationships between, for instance, form and colour, and by linking these features into clusters. Ramachandran and Hirstein argue that a certain part of the brain linked to vision, the extrastriate visual areas, may have evolved specifically to extract such correlations and to unite them into clusters through connections with limbic structures of the brain, that is, some of the evolutionary oldest part of the brain (ibid.). Furthermore, due to the constraints on attention, the authors subsequently propose that art is most appealing if it produces increased activity in only one dimension; either due to only the peak shift effect or the grouping principle. Additionally, they propose another five principles and claim that these principles underlie all forms of experiences with art. It is the final connecting – or the process of "binding" in the more formal language of psychophysics – of the visual features together into a perceptual unit that leads to the sensation of pleasure, they suggest. It is a direct and physiologically based pleasure (ibid.: 22).

Ramachandran and Hirstein attempt to isolate factors that can identify an object as a work of art, and also the biological mechanisms that make individuals respond to these artworks (ibid.). The critiques of the above proposed heuristics, and this reductionistic way of viewing art in particular, are many (see for instance peer commentaries by Martindale 1999; Mitter 1999) and are critiques that reach the whole of the psycho-physical tradition that views art appreciation as something that solely arises from humans' "natural" biological constitution. Even though biological factors influence what we perceive and how we perceive, it is highly unlikely that a theory of biological factors alone is sufficient to account for the appreciation of art.

4.2 Art Understanding

To view the concept of art understanding as a unitary phenomenon is a complex matter. As shown earlier, a variety of phenomena have been considered cognition and many of these are involved in the experience of art known as "art understanding". The central tenet of the theories that explicitly or implicitly lead to art understanding as a form of art experience, however, is that cognition is essential for the experience of art. Cognition is complex, though, and consists of varied phenomena that include such disparate and ambiguous processes as visual perception, categorisation, reasoning, imagining and understanding. Although the different theories of experiences with art have different overarching theoretical frameworks, they have some common characteristics. Various forms of cognition actively organise the experiences of art, and novel information, understanding and cognitive abilities in general can be obtained and enhanced therewith. Funch proposes that art understanding may lead to a feeling of pleasure, but it is a qualitatively different kind of pleasure from the aesthetic pleasure proposed within the psycho-physical tradition. The pleasure is a consequence of cognitive processes, such as "sudden insight", and is therefore only indirectly derived from any features or characteristics of the art work (ibid.).

Since experience with art as "art understanding" has been developed from rather divergent schools of thought with only few common traits, several main approaches will be outlined briefly and separately, according to Funch's delineation.

4.2.1 Perception of the "Good Gestalt"
According to Kurt Koffka, one of the most influential gestalt psychologists of the 20th century, perception is a creative act, wherein one attempts to arrange input into images of "balance and symmetry". Within a work of art, it is the unified perception of "the coherent whole" – the gestalt – that makes people appreciate it, he contends. Such a gestalt can be comprised of the art work's expressive features and reveal a new reality, as perceived by the artist. The appreciation takes the form of profound engagement with this "reality", facilitated by the "good gestalt" of the work of art. It is an individual's mood and characteristics that lead to the appreciation of different kinds of pictures. Along a similar line, Rudolf Arnheim contends in his influential book *Art and Visual Perception* that the perception of art strengthens the "perceptual component", and that a well-developed perception is a necessary precondition for all kinds of thinking (1974). This is the reason Funch regards Koffka's outline as a representation of art understanding (Funch 1997). Gestalt theory as a basis for art appreciation has been further developed by Arnheim, but then extends into the emotional realm, and Funch therefore regards his account as a better representation of emotional experiences with art than of art understanding (ibid.). Arnheim's account is briefly outlined in section 4.3.1 below

4.2.2 Experience of "Pictorial Representation"

Ernst Gombrich, one of the most celebrated art theorists of the 20th century, argues for cognition as a main feature of the appreciation of paintings (1975, 1995). Understanding is never finite and is closely linked to patterns of visual thinking, he claims. Visual thinking is based upon knowledge of the history of art's traditions and the utilization of this knowledge. Individual and collective preferences vary according to the concerns and questions of their time, and if one does not have a relationship to the history of art's changing character, experiences of art have little to offer. The artistic canons are indispensable in that they present points of reference and standards of excellence against which contemporary art can be measured. The meanings of canons, however, are deeply enmeshed with our civilisation, leaving it impossible to discuss them on their own accord. Civilisation, Gombrich argues, can only be transmitted, not directly taught. Our attitudes toward the canons can best be conveyed implicitly, through the way in which we speak about them, or through the way we, in awe, avoid doing so. Funch argues that Gombrich views the perception of art as perception that occurs through mental sets, or schema, that have been developed through experiences with art and which create a framework for expectations and evaluations (1997). Gombrich's view, however, lacks explanations for why people seek to understand art and the psychological meanings of their encounters with art. Instead, he has developed a psychology of the development and of the comprehension of artistic style.

Although Gombrich emphasises understanding and cultural knowledge as a basis for the appreciation of art, he also extends appreciation beyond such phenomena (1975, 1995). He contends that all arts "send their roots deep down into the common ground of universal human response" (1975: 46), yet the level of achievement in a meeting with art is measured through improved understanding. Understanding, again, is reliant upon one's awareness of the history of art's traditions. Gombrich proposes that early conditioning of anticipation and reactions can explain why now-acknowledged masterpieces were once ignored or rejected. Their newness did not permit contemporary modes of visual thinking to comprehend and appraise them.

4.2.3 Experience of Artistic Symbols

According to Gardener, art appreciation consists in the "reading" of artistic symbols. Artistic symbols, he claims, are related to the satisfaction of fundamental, psychoanalytically-based drives and their various ways of functioning. Such "reading", a cognitive act, can lead to various feelings, such as "feelings of pleasure, openness, balance, renewal, penetration, or pathos" (Garderer; cited in Funch 1997: 87). These feelings may be enhanced, in turn, by cognition. In opposition to the philosopher Nelson Goodman, from whose writings his position developed, Gardener contends that emotions are of main importance and are ends in themselves. Goodman seemed to give emotions secondary importance and argued that emotions provide a basis for cognition and can enhance understanding (Funch 1997).

4.2.4 A Developmental Perspective

Michael Parsons attempts to empirically develop a universal stage theory of the aesthetic experience; he tries to categorise people's understanding of art into a developmental sequence (1987). Toward this end, he classifies people's answers according to their type of reasoning when discussing five or six paintings. The subjects were to describe the pictures while their personal experiences with them were only indirectly investigated. Parsons and his co-workers conducted over three hundred semi-structured interviews over a ten-year period, throughout which the theory was constantly revised according to data. Five distinct stages appeared. These are not associated with age but with people's experiences with art. Parsons' results suggested that at the first stage, the understanding of the work of art, briefly stated, is based upon immediate responses according to favourite objects. For example, a person at this stage may like the work of art because it contains his or her favourite colour. Differently, the most mature mode of understanding art is essentially a stage wherein the individual evaluates the art work's meaning according to cultural frameworks for interpreting works of art while at the same time being aware and critical of the "values" and "concepts" inherent in this framework (ibid.: 25). Understanding of the art work is based upon individuals' relative autonomous judgments that are shaped in dialogue with others. According to Parsons, understanding of a work of art is reflected in people's interpretation of the art work's subject matter, expression, medium, form and style as well as in the kind of judgement involved. Differing approaches to these topics form various ways of understanding art, he contends. Funch, however, underscores that Parsons also considers art understanding to involve investigations into the nature of the self and what it means to be human.

4.2.5 A Neuro-Aesthetic Approach
A neuro-aesthetic approach to art does not necessarily exclude a cognitive approach to art appreciation. For instance, neuroscientist Semir Zeki contends that "the function of art" is to facilitate a search for essential and abiding features (1999). From such exploration one acquires the possibility to generalise about objects and to "acquire knowledge about a wide category of objects and faces" (ibid: 79); one obtains a certain kind of understanding and information about the world. Appreciation of art occurs when the search for constancies is sated to some extent, Zeki contends.

4.2.6 Summary
These are the main ways in which art understanding has been treated within institutionalised psychology. The psychological consequences of art understanding have never been abundantly investigated, however, and little emphasis is generally given to emotions and motivation, as well as to other psychological features. The next section deals with emotions as elicited by experiences with art.

4.3 Emotional Appreciation
Experiences of emotions have frequently been posited as essential features of a meeting with art, but no one has developed a comprehensive theory of emotional responses. The main investigations within psychology of emotional responses to art come from the tradition of Gestalt Psychology (Funch 1997). Recently, emotion and art have come under scrutiny in the work of Derek Matravers and in the anthology by Mette Hjort and Sue Laver, but these works mainly focus upon philosophical, rather than psychological aspects, and have, therefore, not been included in this selection (Matravers 1998; Hjort and Laver 1997). Additionally, empirical studies of emotional experiences to art works have been scarce. What follows are synopses of the few focal attributions of the descriptions of emotional experiences with art. Based on these, Funch summarises emotional experiences with art as an immediate reaction

to expressive features of a work of art. It is a kind of experience wherein a particular emotion is felt toward the work of art, prior to conscious cognition or thought taking place. Frequently, the particular emotion is accompanied by an additional feeling of pleasure, but it is a pleasure of a more sanguine nature.

4.3.1 Rudolf Arnheim

Funch considers Arnheim's approach to art appreciation an emotional one. Arnheim investigates psychological processes involved in the creation and perception of art (1974). His considerations are based upon gestalt theory of visual perception whereby he regards vision as primarily the perception of gestalts. A gestalt forms the basis for perception wherein basic components appear as a coherent whole, without individual parts. The perception of gestalts occurs immediately and automatically, prior to any conscious knowledge, he contends. Perception of gestalts is based upon general gestalt principles as well as upon individual characteristics and cultural climates. In regard to art, it is the appearance of dynamic and expressive elements that leads to appreciation. In Arnheim's aforementioned seminal book *Art and Visual Perception,* he exposes characteristics of visual perception. Different rules and features form gestalts that can take numerous forms and lead to expressiveness within works of art.

Generally, it is the experience of the expressive aspects that leads to the appreciation of art, and any recognition of emotions, for instance, is secondary. Art has unique possibilities for the creation of expression, since the artist has complete control over the work of art. Thus art can contain expressions that represent the manifold of experience in daily existence more clearly than can ordinary ways of living.

Arnheim identifies two main opposing, yet complimentary, "forces" within the human psyche. One strives toward simplicity and order, the other toward discrepancy and disorder. The former provides a basis for comprehension, understanding and meaning-creation. The latter facilitates for continued growth and expansion. A work of art contains both forces, which leads to psychic "tension". In view of that, Arnheim does not use the terms "emotions" or "feelings" as results of experiences of the expressive aspects of art works, but "tensions". Differing kinds of tensions are related to differing kinds of subject matter and the work of art's various forms of expressiveness. Funch considers this kind of art appreciation an emotional one, because he views the tension that Arnheim proposes as closely related to emotions.

4.3.2 Aesthetic Emotions

Jerrold Levinson identifies several main questions in regard to the broad topics of art and emotion, one being whether there is a specific type of emotion involved in experiences with art – a so-called "aesthetic emotion" (1997). Several attempts have been made to describe such an aesthetic emotion, but none has been fully identified and accepted. Different emotions may also be experienced when viewing works of art, but these are of secondary importance and are only "side effects" of art appreciation. The German psychologist Theodor Lipps is maybe the most historically prominent theoretician to have expanded upon an account of aesthetic emotions (Funch 1997).

    Lipps considers art appreciation to be strongly associated with the experience of empathy. He defines aesthetic empathy as an emotion wherein the viewer experiences emotions that are attributed to the object's experience as parts of himself/herself. Such aesthetic empathy is associated with aesthetic pleasure. Pleasure can take on many different forms, however, depending upon the situation in which it is experienced. General features of such pleasure are that the experience of the subject/object distinction has dissolved and that the viewer has no experience of self-identity. Aesthetic pleasure, Lipps claims, compliments the experience of aesthetic empathy and has the virtue of being experienced as glorious and untainted, with vast individual significance, differing with each work of art. Such an experience of art appears as an isolated event; the art object seems to exist in a sphere of its own. Only the automatic use of tools for contemplation, such as language and knowledge of shapes and forms, are employed. The emotions experienced are dependent upon the already established emotional repertoire of the viewer and are not seen as mainly functions of bodily-based sensations, i.e. they are of a more mental nature. The empathy experienced is elicited by the art work's form and not by its content, Lipps contends. The form, consisting of pleasurable gestalts, gives vitality to the art object and facilitates for the experience of empathy and pleasure (Funch 1997).

Other psychological researchers mention emotional aspects of art experiences as well, but here emotions take on a radically different form. In all the various schools of thought, as delineated by Funch, emotion, broadly defined, plays a role, albeit not always a primary, defining one. In the psycho-physical tradition, the sensation of pleasure is the *sine qua non*, yet it remains contentious as to whether the pleasure involved is an actual emotion. Researchers like Gombrich, Gardener and Parsons within the cognitive traditions, view emotions as inchoate. Within the psychoanalytic tradition, cathartic pleasure is what leads to the appreciation of art, the pleasure being a function of the catharsis. From the existential-phenomenological point of view, experience with art is of primary importance; in a meeting with art, diffuse emotions are given significant form.

4.4 Aesthetic Fascination
Aesthetic fascination is a kind of experience with art described by psychoanalytic schools of thought. This fascination is proposed as being in play for both the creator and the viewer, as Freud and other prominent psychoanalysts do not differentiate between experiences of the artist and of the viewer, claiming that these experiences are, in fact, identical. The same underlying psychical processes are at play, they contend. Freud's writings on art appreciation per se have been scarce, but his indirect viewpoints can be expounded upon based on his writings on the activity of the artist.

4.4.1 Cathartic Pleasure
A Freudian assumption is that the artist sublimates or transforms threatening themes into consciously unrecognisable content in the work of art, leading to transformation of unacceptable desires for the viewer as well. Cathartic effects, wherein trapped energy finds means of release through sublimation, with the consequent release of tension, lead to the sensation of pleasure. The art work may continue to elicit such cathartic responses with consequent intense pleasure, eliciting enduring fascination with the work of art (Funch 1997).

There is some internal tension within the various brands of psychoanalytic thought and varying emphasis is placed on differing features by different theorists. Ronald Fairbairn claims that an aesthetic experience occurs when viewing an art object activates certain unconscious affective demands of the id – the basic, uncensored mental force (1938: 173). Fairbairn contends that destructive impulses and subsequent guilt-easing wishes of restitution are frequently incorporated into works of art. Appreciation of such a work occurs when the work of art contains a perceived sense of integrity. This integrity facilitates for emotional discharge of unconscious fantasies of obliteration and amendment, echoing the drives for destruction and restitution in the artist (Funch 1997). Hana Segal has a distinct psychoanalytic approach to experiences with art as she distinguishes between cathartic pleasures, which arise from the discharge of unconscious tension, and accompanying "associative" emotions that together form aesthetic appreciation. These emotions are derived from the work of art's content and its "significant form"[2], and both are imbued with unconscious emotional significance. Ernst Kris argues that art may be appreciated based upon its formal structures and perceived meaning which are mediated through its cultural context as well as through the psyche of the individual viewer. It is an active discovery which may result in a gradual process of tension discharge through a curtailed release of distinctions between conscious and unconscious processes. Kris describes this process of art appreciation as one where the theme of the art work is recognised and becomes assimilated into existing structures of the psyche. The differentiation between the subject and the object dissipates and the object becomes engrained in the viewer. This occurs as the ego, the main mediator between various internal and external forces, loosens its control. The ego regains its previous level of control over the id, however, and, at the same time, the viewer can experience the creation of the effects within the art work and align himself/herself with the artist. Kris believes that the shifts in the differing degrees of control between these psychic functions are in themselves pleasurable (Funch 1997: 166-167).

These different psychoanalytically-developed theories of experiences with art have the common conception that experiences with art serve a cathartic function that is pleasurable and that may lead to the phenomenon of long-term fascination with a work of art. It may be that other emotional responses accompany the experience, but

---

[2] Clive Bell developed the notion of "significant form" (1913/1961: 37). He contends that that "to appreciate a work of art we need bring with us nothing from life, no knowledge of its ideas and affairs, no familiarity with its emotions". Art works are defined by having "significant form", a feature that one inherently appreciates.

arguably these are subdued due to the intense experience of pleasure (Funch 1997).

4.4.2 A Jungian Perspective

From a Jungian perspective, Erich Neumann diminishes the role of cathartic pleasure, describing a rather different (psycho) analytic approach to art appreciation. He underscores the importance of the collective unconscious as being a preconscious and ontological, or primary, reality that lends organization and power to "ego-consciousness". Art appreciation occurs within The Great Experience: the individual surpasses the foundational features of the set of archetypes; symbolic images common to "the timeless radiant dynamic that is at the hearth of the world" (Funch 1997: 183). Experiences with art can elicit such transcendence by initiating movement of archetypal symbols. When the "great experience" occurs, the art work is revealed as being part of a timeless sphere. It is described as a supernatural experience wherein distinctions between the viewer and the subject dissipate and divinity is revealed. Emotions are deeper within this experience and of an unusual intensity, ending in a most fulfilling and beautiful state where the essence of being can be sensed but not comprehended, which Funch proposes may lead to a continued fascination with the work of art that elicited the experience (Funch 1997).

4.5 The Aesthetic Experience

Funch has arrived at this conceptualisation of the aesthetic experience through existential-phenomenological lines of thought. Philosophically, this tradition has roots in Søren Kierkegaard, Edmund Husserl and Martin Heidegger. Heidegger's lecture, *The Origin of the Work of Art* is likely to be one of the first existential-phenomenological investigations into the nature of art (1935/2003). Here Heidegger explores the meaning and truth of works of art, including how works of art make truth open to experience.

4.5.1 Phenomenological Psychology

Within phenomenological psychology there are some studies which look into concrete experiences with art. Bulloch is one who conducts such a study (1912; cited in Funch 1997). He investigates what he calls "aesthetic consciousness", and argues that psychological distance is an essential part of aesthetic experience. He contends that there is no universal pleasure involved in the aesthetic encounter, but that there is a particular aesthetic consciousness, characterised by its intent contemplation that fills the senses. The subject/object distinction appears diminished, yet not lost. There is a peculiar kind of distance between the ego and its regular content, wherein the art work "stands outside the context of our personal needs and ends" (Bulloch 1912; cited in Funch 1997: 192). Another study has been conducted by Csikszentmihalyi and Robinson (1990). They underscore experiences with art as an end in itself. It involves a fadeout of self-consciousness, including a lack of awareness of one's own identity; it is a heightened awareness of the act itself wherein the individual and the art work appear as a world unto their own. Only after the episode has ended is one able to reflect upon it. Then it is viewed as an intensely satisfying experience, thereby contributing to one's overall life quality. Csikszentmihalyi has named such experiences "flow experiences" (1992, 1997). After phenomenological interviews of museum professionals, he and Robinson (1990) came to the conclusion that art experiences also could take such forms. In contrast to other flow experiences, however, one can discriminate between its structure and content, they contend. The structure is universal and takes the form of the flow experience while the content is related to the particular work of art and the particular approach of each individual viewer (Funch 1997). Rollo May outlines psychological forces in the act of creating art, including its existential importance based upon phenomenological observations and considerations. He regards works of art as manifesting existential dilemmas of their time and experiences with art as increasing personal integrity. With these historical antecedents, Funch conceptualises what he terms "the aesthetic experience" (1997).

The aesthetic experience is a relatively rare occurrence and is described as transcendental, only to be experienced in relation to artistic objects. It can be identified as a "leap of consciousness", where the experience has no other goal than itself and is of a unique emotional character. The individual is deeply engaged in a picture which seems to be of a translucent character. It is the visual qualities of the object, along with its existential content, that create opportunities for such an experience. In order for an individual to have "the aesthetic experience", he or she needs to be "emotionally ready", which is something that can only be achieved through life experience.

In other words, one's emotional life needs some kind of maturity to meet the issues manifested in works of art.

Although the aesthetic experience is a rare occurrence, it has the possibility of giving rise to core emotional change. Emotions, Funch argues, have in themselves no significant shape; they exist in vague and amorphous forms until they are given points of reference. When emotions do not have a distinct form, one is not able to relate to one's own feelings. A contemporary picture, which manifests the existential dilemmas of its time, creates the ideal situation in which an individual's undifferentiated emotion can be given a "distinct form". Through such metamorphosis into a full- blown form, the emotion can be incorporated into the psyche. Such incorporation of an emotion lends room to reflect upon the emotion, as well as to facilitate a stabilisation of one's emotional life. Emotional stress is thus alleviated (Funch 1997, 2000).

There are three main descriptive features of the aesthetic experience which can be described: the intentional, the visual, and the emotional -all seem to possess unusual qualities. Moreover, the entire overarching relationship between cognition and emotion seems imbued with unusual characteristics.

4.5.2 Features of the Aesthetic Experience

Contrary to everyday experiences where intentionality or attention is frequently directed toward future acts, the focus of this experience is all-pervading and an end in itself. Past and future acts are of no relevance, yet there is no "loss of ego". A sense of self and a sense of individuality ground the experience, but also remain on the periphery of it. The individual is vigorously, but covertly, involved in converting existential problems into new solutions. The way one perceives the external world within the aesthetic experience appears extraordinary. The perception is of unusual clarity and contains several unique characteristics; the image appears to hold a remarkable radiance, lending a sublime dimension to the experience. The image appears to have a visual unity, eliciting experiences of familiarity and uniqueness simultaneously. Cognition may exist in the form of immediate detection, which is not an outcome of active cognition, but rather of "direct perception". This impulsive and unstructured recognition consists of an effortless identification of the topic(s) with its underlying existential thesis. The cognitive aspects take a passive and non-invasive stance with no other cognitive act than this immediate recognition; there are no present thoughts (Funch 1997). Thus the degree to which cognition is involved in vision determines the extent to which cognition is involved in the aesthetic experience. Cognition here is minimal compared to other experiences and, as such, this view emulates the Zajonc-Lazarus debate.

    Within the aesthetic experience there are variations among the kinds of emotional feelings elicited, but they do have several corresponding characteristics. They are of an overwhelming nature, not limited or controlled by conscious cognition or any other factors; they are experienced in their full, raw expression, penetrating the entire state of being. They are new emotions, different from all previous ones, and are given full form in this meeting with the work of art, although this aspect may not appear conscious to the person experiencing it. The experience of the emotion is one that is "new, overpowering, and pleasurable". As a result of such experience, the emotion exists in a new and pure form that may shape later emotional and cognitive maturity. The cognitive aspect of the emotion or feeling is of a unique kind, where the emotion exists as an overwhelming force, containing and eliciting no cognitive organization of knowledge.

    How do these emotional experiences vary within the aesthetic experience? Different works of art contain different existential themes and, accordingly, give rise to a range of emotions. Thus the defining feature of the aesthetic experience is the structural organisation described above, while the emotions elicited may be of various kinds.

4.6 Art Appreciation and "Embodied Imagination"
Joy and Sherry focus on rather different features of experiences with art, namely the experience of art as "embodied imagination" (2003). In their investigation they uphold the primacy of the body in coming to grips with experience and exemplify it through people's experience with art. In the course of analysing "consumption stories" of museum goers, Joy and Sherry support Maurice Merleau-Ponty's notion of the body and its actions as principal for meaningful experience (Merleau-Ponty 1945/1962), decentring the notion of an abstracted and separated mind as proposed by the French philosopher René Descartes. From an existential-phenomenological angle, founded in Merleau-Ponty's philosophical investigations, Joy and Sherry

illustrate how embodiment of experience may occur at a phenomenal level. Then with tools for the analysis of metaphors, they investigate embodiment within the cognitive unconscious; through people's somatic experiences with art, the role of embodiment in processes of unconscious cognition within experiences with art is explored, leading to descriptions of relationships between various works of art and peoples' bodily movements in relation to them.

To my knowledge, this study is the first one that empirically investigates the role of the body in experiences with art. As such it is an important investigation. However, Joy and Sherry are seemingly unaware of Funch's work, and their own lacks categorisation according to various experiential dimensions. Such classification would lead to a more refined depiction of the process of embodiment as it occurs in different kinds of experiences with art. Moreover, the role of emotion in both the experience of art as well as in the process of embodiment is subdued. They implicitly make emotions into cognitive events, because a cognitive act to them is "any mental operation of multisensory and neural processing" (ibid: 4). However, their empirical work is apparently the first of its kind and provides a sound basis for further investigation into the role of embodiment in the experience of art, the phenomenological unit of experience and the relative importance of the overlapping but disparate phenomena of emotion and cognition.

4.7 Experiences of Art as a Contemplation of Signs

Kjørup has conducted a philosophical investigation into central questions of art and aesthetics, wherein a relationship between emotion and cognition is outlined (2000). He contends there are many kinds of meetings with works of art and identifies several varieties of understanding and awareness that may be obtained in these meetings. A picture's features, structure, content and meaning, from its singular parts to its collected theme, can engender different kinds of knowledge. At a fundamental level, an encounter offers information about the specific work. At a more universal level, it can offer information about technical features of paintings in general, such as the use of materials and methods. Directly and indirectly a painting can contain statements or messages, such as ethical instructions or existential considerations. The directly expressed thesis, however, frequently becomes commonplace and trite, while a latent meaning tends to be more unique, and often veiled within the form of the work. Most importantly, though, a work of art contains meaning, which extends beyond the work itself. Construction of meaning can take the form of revelation and clarification of fascinating topics, such as variations within and between historical epochs, and portrayals of different personalities engaged in diverse human relations. The individual actively participates in such revelations which, in turn, generate opportunities for reflection and discussion – that are both pleasurable and provide applicable knowledge.

The aesthetic experience upon which Kjørup expounds he deems pragmatic, wherein the individual is actively engaged, both emotionally and intellectually. Attention is focused on essential features of the work of art, and the experience is enhanced through background knowledge as well as practical facilitation of correct lighting, for example. Another feature of the aesthetic experience is that it is an end in itself; our experience of it is devoid of interest in secondary gains. The traditional distance between object and subject is diminished in that the experience consists of lively participation. The viewer dynamically considers the signs of the artwork, not because of what they can reveal, but because of their inherent, interesting qualities.

In the aesthetic experience, there is no longer a dichotomy between feelings and thought,[3] Kjørup claims. Feelings play a causal role in thought as feelings allegedly direct our attention toward essential features of the painting that are necessary for a profound experience of it. He suggests that almost any kind and strength of feeling can play the role of guiding attention except for maybe really strong feelings. The direction of attention, however, does not occur solely because of feelings, but also due to intellectual considerations (Kjørup 2000).

Kjørup gives examples of the considerable role that feelings play in meetings with art via memories of such. Seldom does one

---

[3] Kjørup writes in Danish and uses the terms "følelse" and "erkendelse". "Følelse" seems to denote the English terms "feeling" and "emotion" without significant differentiation. The term "erkjendelse" does not have an English equivalent, but is generally acknowledged as referring to complex phenomena such as recognising, realization and cognition (according to Gyldendal's Danish to English Dictionary, 1995).

remember a unitary picture, but a unitary feeling arises nonetheless. The work of art may become clear through the development of this feeling. Moreover, he gives the example of Da Vinci's *La Gioconda*, the painting known as *Mona Lisa,* and demonstrates how his aesthetic experience leads to a more profound meeting with this popular picture.

In conclusion, Kjørup explicates the aesthetic experience as one of emotional and cognitive effort, where signs are contemplated for their intrinsic worth and not as means to an end. Feelings function to direct attention, and the experience takes place within the practical sphere. He thereby challenges historical and contemporary views of the aesthetic experience, especially the notion of it being one of immediacy. Such immediacy, he claims, is manifested in Bulloch's psychical distance, Lipps' aesthetic empathy and Kant's disinterested pleasure; all attempts to describe the aesthetic experience.

4.8 Experiences of Art as a Hermeneutical Endeavour
The erudite scholar Hans-Georg Gadamer's interpretation of the aesthetic encounter takes form from Heidegger's phenomenological concept of the hermeneutical circle and his philosophical work on the nature of art. Based upon such historical antecedents, Gadamer proposes that experiences with art are closely linked to processes of understanding (1960/1989, 1977/1986). He postulates that understanding occurs in a hermeneutical "circle". This circle is a continuous experiential process of mental oscillation between observing the parts and the whole. Neither is understandable alone as the whole is given meaning through its parts and vice versa. Such a hermeneutical circle is not separable into finite phenomena that can be exposed to scientific investigation, but is fundamental to the way experience occurs. As such it is characteristic of our meeting with works of art.

A meeting with a work of art is experienced as a passive act, where the art work's "truth" is foisted upon the viewer. It is a "game" in which the viewer becomes absorbed. Current conceptions and ways of understanding form the basis of how one interprets a work of art, while improved understanding is fostered through hermeneutical movements between observing the work of art with its parts and whole. A conversation about the meaning of the work of art is thus created. Preconceived notions may hinder the understanding of the work's claim to truth, but the work of art questions these assumptions. A "fusion of horizons" may occur when the viewer experiences the work of art, changing or substantiating the preconceived notions. In such meetings with works of art, interpretations lead to a mediation of the understanding of one's self through the incorporation of a different or new perspective. Self understanding, however, always resides within historical conditions, which is partly why self-understanding is never finite, but hermeneutical.

In his later writings Gadamer claims that one is in a "reciprocal game" with works of art. Through a meeting with art, our ways of thinking are confronted and improved. This, in turn, challenges art to respond to our transformed state of mind. As we are altered in a meeting with art, our perception of the art work's "claim to truth" is transformed, creating new questions to which art works must respond. The art work's answer, then, contains possibilities for improved self-understanding (Wright 1998).

The first part of Gadamer's magnum opus *Truth and Method* involves a rejection of the philosopher Immanuel Kant's notion of disinterested pleasure. Kant's argument, briefly stated, is that the experience of beauty and art[4] is based upon on an inherent capacity to experience pleasure when viewing such (1790/1997). The pleasure experienced in such instances is not sensuous, but intellectual. According to the Kantian view, experience with art leads to an ahistorical individual pleasure, Gadamer contends. Gadamer's work can be said, then, to involve a rejection of narrow conceptions of aesthetic experiences that are, for instance, limited to the experience of pleasure, such as within the psychophysical tradition. Rather, aesthetic experiences elicit new modes of understanding and are historically situated dialogues between the art and the viewer. It may, therefore, be a distinct delineation of art appreciation close to Funch's cognitive kind.

It seems as though Gadamer indirectly limits the role of emotion in understanding one's historical situated-ness. As Kant rejects "taste as [having] any *significance as knowledge*" (Gadamer 1989: 43, original italicisation), Gadamer discards understanding having significance as emotional. He appears to highlight improved reason and understanding as essential features of experiences with art

---

[4] According to Kant art is "The presentation of aesthetic ideas" (Gadamer 1989: p. 52).

at the expense of emotional ones. In one passage, however, he states that understanding is "a part of the event in which meaning occurs, the event in which the meaning of all statements – those of art and all other kinds of tradition – is formed and actualised (Gadamer 1989: 165). It seems as though understanding would have to be a part of any event that elicits truths and arguably would have to be included in events that are emotional. Moreover, it may be that Gadamer uses "understanding" in its broadest sense: to include emotional and other psychical "events".

One can view Funch's aesthetic experience, however, as explaining parts of a hermeneutical process. Through the aesthetic experience the viewer becomes emotionally transformed, creating new existential dilemmas to which works of art may respond. Funch's delineation of aesthetic experiences is limited to psychological theories and does not expound on Gadamer's interpretation of aesthetic experiences, although both theses are founded on the early phenomenologist's work. The tension between Funch's emotionally effective aesthetic experience and Gadamer's emphasis on understanding in experiences with art underscores tensions between emotion and cognition and their relative importance/merging in self-understanding and meaning-creation. With the authors' respective historical interpretation of aesthetic experiences, their differences in viewing the nature of emotion and cognition colour their perception of the experience of art. Within the current zeitgeist of investigations into the seemingly separate, but overlapping, domains of emotion and cognition, further conceptualisations of aesthetic experiences and the influence of these experiences on human existence, may continue and ripen.

It may be that the relationship between cognition and emotion will alter with different forms of art as well as within different genres of painting. This study has been limited to people's experience of visual art – mostly pictures, but also installation art. Research into shifting relationships between emotion and cognition has been conducted in regard to experiences with film. Grodal conducts an evolutionary-based investigation into emotional and cognitive processes involved in different genres of film (1997, 2003). Through an analysis founded upon an evolutionary point of view, he contends that different genres of film elicit different responses according to our common biological constitution. I agree with Helles and Køppe's critique of the use of neurobiology as a foundation for analysis of experiences with film (1999). Experiences of film occur at a phenomenal level, with correlating neural responses. For such a theory to hold, Grodal will need to explain how phenomenal experience can be neurological properties – not a simple task to be sure. Currently biological correlates can be investigated independently, but cannot form the basis of a theory of the experiential level of film. Thus, as this is a thesis about experiences with art at the phenomenal level, no usage of Grodal's work will take place. An extensive critique of his work can be found in Helles and Køppe (ibid.).

Gadamer claims that art lends unique means for the discovery of truth. Although method is presented as "no crude antithesis to truth" through the stringent use of method, such truths may be concealed or ignored (Bernasconi 1986: xii). Nevertheless, the next chapter comprises a psychological-phenomenological investigation, including a usage of their methods, in an attempt to facilitate understanding.

Chapter 5
A Phenomenological Study of Art Appreciation

The topic of study in this chapter is the manifestations of cognition in emotions at a phenomenal level, and experiences with art were chosen as a vehicle for such expressions. The review of literature on art appreciation was conducted in the previous chapter, and shows that in art appreciation emotion and cognition, and their relationship(s), have been theorised to have a variety of forms. What follows is a study of peoples' actual experiences of this relationship in an attempt to describe experiences of emotion as well as explore the possibility of distinguishing between emotions and cognition. Some of the methods of phenomenological psychology are used to uncover aspects of the cognitive-emotive relationship.

5.1 Methodology
Esbjerg museum of art agreed to facilitate interviews of their museum public. It is a modern art museum that has embraced contemporary psychological theories of art appreciation, thereby enhancing the visitors' experiences. For instance, in the permanent collection no information about the art works is given next to the pictures; a procedure not frequently employed at museums, but which lends focus to the artworks themselves and their own power of expression. The museum contains mainly Danish art of the 20th century, with a focus upon current art. At the time of the study, the museum featured two contemporary exhibitions. One was an installation containing two works by Olafur Eliasson called *Surroundings Surrounded* (2001) and *Light Extension* (2002) in which he changes the perception of the museum rooms via lights and mirrors, among other. Katya Sanders and Andrea Geyer had created the other installation: Two labyrinths with projections of an airport with short bits of texts. This work was titled *Meaning is What Hides the Instability of Ones Position* (2004) and was a cooperation between the Danish and the German artist, respectively. This is an annual feature of the museum, wherein a Danish artist is invited to create a work with their chosen artist from a different country. The museum also featured parts of their permanent collection, an aesthetic laboratory where pictures and sculptures can

be manipulated and played with, as well as a sculpture garden. The permanent collection contains mainly painted pictures, but also photographs, sculptures and ceramics. Additionally, the parts of the permanent collection not displayed are hung on movable walls that can be pulled out and viewed by the visitors.

5.1.1 Interview Guide

In order to make possible the uncovering of areas and nuances not anticipated from the outset, a relatively open interview structure was preferred with much room for the participants to define the interview. Steinar Kvale's semi-structured interview was chosen as the preferred interview style (1997). As inferred by the title, the interview is partially organized. Moreover, it covers a middle ground of qualitative research methods, as it is neither inductive, i.e. completely open and based upon the appearing unstructured data alone, nor hesitant to acknowledge the subjectivity of the researcher.

5.1.2 Procedure

Taped interviews were conducted for four days. Ten interviews were made with a total of thirteen people about their experiences with art. As this was a qualitative interview, it was the quality and not the number of interviews that determined the extent of the investigation. Four interviews were already planned before the interviewer arrived at the museum. The remaining six interviews were conducted with people who happened to visit the museum. Some of these people were asked by the salesperson in the ticket booth if they would be available for a conversation about their experiences at the museum after visiting the exhibits.

Most of the museum visitors were interviewed immediately after their visit to the exhibitions. This occurred in order to ensure that the experiences were still fresh in their minds so that their stories were as rich and accurate as possible. The interviews were conducted in an empty room and in a quiet place in the museum hall. If the interviewees desired, the exhibits were visited again during the interview. At one of the interviewee's request, the interview was conducted at the art studio in which she worked. After the interviews were conducted, impressions from the interviews were immediately written down. Three of the interviewees were German and these interviews were conducted in English. For those people who arrived as couples, both people were present at the interview, but the conversation focused upon the experience of only one of the pair.

Validity and reliability are features that one should attempt to secure from the beginning of the research process. Strauss and Corbin suggest several techniques that increase sensitivity, minimise bias and interpretations of an unwarranted nature (1999). These techniques include continuously asking questions about what the participants say, conducting a microanalysis of words, concepts and statements, making comparisons in order to discuss contrasting statements, as well as reacting to strong and polarised expressions. An attempt was made to follow such criteria throughout the interviews as well as in the process of analysis. Along a similar line, Kvale underscores that the interview should ideally be interpreted throughout the interview process so that an interpersonal consensus is reached about the meanings involved (1997). This requires the interviewer to extract essential themes from the interview, evaluate what these themes involve, and give the participant feedback about how what has been said is being analysed and understood, so that the participants can react and adjust the interviewer's interpretations.

5.1.3 Analysis
Eight interviews were selected for transcription and analysis, based upon the criteria of language fluency and richness of description. In the first meeting with the interview material, the primary task completed was to read through the interviews. This was conducted in order to obtain a sense of the nature of the data material. Then, an attempt was made to put together the immediate impressions of the data material. This was conducted through a "brain storming" process, or a relatively uncensored description of what appeared as important themes or categories.

From these first processes, the data material presented itself as somewhat extensive and impenetrable. Therefore, the data material was condensed for meaning according to Kvale's method for meaning condensation (1997). Through such analysis, one arrives at a brief description or formulation of the participant's expressed opinions; one obtains an overview over the participant's perspective. It compresses the material and makes it more comprehensible. This condensation of meaning was conducted in several steps. First, the "natural units of meaning" as they appeared expressed by the participants were highlighted. Then, the theme that dominated each unit was described as simply as possible. Finally, each unit of meaning was investigated according to whether they could inform the topic of investigation. From the condensation of meaning, several differences and similarities became evident in regards to the participant's appreciation of art and the manifestation of the relationship between cognition and emotion. These findings are discussed in the results sections. Then, an analysis of metaphors, relevant to the pertinent questions, was conducted. Through an analysis of metaphors, one acquires insights into the cognitive unconscious (Joy and Sherry 2003). In other words, knowledge can be obtained about how the participants indirectly view emotions, cognition, and the relationship between them, as well as about how they structure these views. The analysis was performed according to George Lakoff and Mark Johnson's as well as Gilles Fauconnier and Mark Turner's framework for interpreting metaphors (Lakoff and Johnson 1980, 1999; Fauconnier and Turner 2002). Their approaches come out of the cognitive-linguistic tradition, explained below, and their work has made important contributions to the understanding of metaphors. There are, however, numerous approaches to the meanings and interpretations of metaphors, and this framework was selected as it, in particular, deals with metaphors in relation to emotions. Within this framework, the use of metaphors is regarded as a cognitive process, whereby one concept, or feature of experience, is understood and given structure by another linguistic expression. Moreover, according to Johnson "(...) metaphors are pervasive, irreducible, imaginative structures of human understanding that influence the nature of meaning and constrain our rational inferences" (1987: xii). A stronger claim postulated by Lakoff and Johnson is that "our ordinary conceptual system, in which we both think and act, is fundamentally metaphorical in nature" (1980: 3). Metaphors are, thus, in this latter strongest claim, the underlying feature of our way of being in the world – the underlying feature of both thinking and acting.

In the above framework, metaphors can be analysed and categorised into distinct kinds. Some of the most relevant kinds in relation to emotion are primary metaphors, complex metaphors and their conglomeration in "conceptual blends". Primary metaphors are metaphors that originate from associations between experience and one's environment. Complex metaphors lack this immediate grounding in experience, but consist of a fusion of primary metaphors (Lakoff and Johnson 1999). In brief, conceptual blending is a complex model wherein a "target domain" (the phenomenon being explained) is given structure from a less abstract concept. The target domain and the source domain, the less abstract concept, share a "generic space" where the structures they share are described. Then, in "the blend", protrusions from the target domain as well as from the generic space are combined. This "blending" results in the target domain being given a new, emergent structure. Such blends can incessantly be created, in a continuous process of metaphorical structuring of "the conceptual system" (Fauconnier and Turner 2002).

The interviews were scrutinised, sentence by sentence, wherefrom essential primary and complex metaphors, as well as conceptual blends, were extracted. Certain metaphors were highly informative and were analysed according to the above-mentioned framework. Results obtained from the investigation of the participant's use of metaphors are also discussed in the findings sections.

5.2 Findings

The findings from this investigation are divided into three sections where the results of the psychological-phenomenological analysis are discussed. From these analyses, the condensation of meaning and analysis of metaphors, several topics appeared that illuminate the relationship between emotion and cognition. These results create the base for what follows thereafter – a general description of various affective states.

5.2.1 Emotions without Conscious Cognition

It is noticeable in several of the interviews that the participants experience affect without the involvement of conscious cognition. Therese, for instance, recalls what she considers to be a great experience with art. She views the decoration of Ishøj Church in Denmark together with two friends. They look at and talk about different features of the decoration, and at one stage they sit down and contemplate it in a more solitary manner. At this point she experiences her thoughts to be minimal; it appears as though the art becomes a part of her in that she is no longer thinking about the object. She relates this experience to the forms and shapes of the decoration; it felt almost god-like to her. She contrasts such experiences to more intellectual experiences with art.

The experiences of Siv underscore the same differentiation between cognitive and non-cognitive experiences. She claims that she has rather different experiences with pictures as compared to three-dimensional objects. When she views pictures, it seems to her that only parts of her are involved. Her thoughts appear more prevalent than any other mental or physiological phenomena. She emphasises her statement by touching her head. In converse to her more cognitive experiences with pictures, she perceives her whole body to be involved when viewing sculptures. Differently, she has experiences with pictures that appear non-cognitive as well. She shows me one of the pictures at the museum with which she has had her most preferable experience. It is a picture by Niels Larsen Stevns (1864-1941), a Danish painter famous for his portrayal of biblical scenes and natural landscapes. This one has a nature motif that appears serene and tranquil. She views the picture every time she visits the museum, and has spent significant time with it at her current visit. When describing her own experience, she explains how she lets her eyes meander and rest without any specific purpose. She claims she has had no awareness of time passing and no thoughts when she viewed it by herself.

A third participant also accentuates that he experiences cognition and emotion as distinct. Kristoffer takes us to the creation *Downward Trend* which he particularly likes. It is made by Nina Saunders, a contemporary Danish artist currently living in London. It is a chair which form appears to have melted somewhat onto the floor. He states that he immediately appreciates it for its originality and funniness, and regards it as containing "complete newness". When he was asked whether it was a thought he had, he corrects the interviewer and states: "No, no, it was a feeling; you know you come in, you look at it, and it was just like 'wow'". He emphasises that his experience of it is one without thought, and it is an immediate "feeling aspect" that makes him appreciate it. When he views a different creation, he compares the two experiences: "I was thinking about this one, more than about that one. That one was just for the feeling, this one was more for the mind, you know, you can see meaning in that if you want". This latter work he likes because of the thoughts it triggers. It makes him curious.

Picture of "Downward Trend" by Nina Saunders. 1998.

"I liked it more for the mind, you know. Not that much for the feeling, but more for the mind", Kristoffer states. With this work, he experiences no feelings or sensations – only thoughts: "I really did not feel anything on this one. I was just thinking". He stresses his perception of having separate cognitive and emotional experiences. To him, these appear as distinct kinds of experiences, whereby different pictures elicit various emotional and cognitive responses. Some reactions he views to be feeling-based, others to be cognitively-founded.

These three examples are the most obvious that show how the participants have subjective experiences, wherein affect and conscious cognition appear as distinct phenomena; they are experienced as dichotomous and different. The participants stress this differentiation, as it contains an important experiential difference for them. From a theoretical stance, as described in chapter two, Lazarus stresses the impossibility of separating emotions from cognition in nature (1999). Zajonc, who refers to conscious cognition, contends that emotions and cognition almost always are intertwined (2000). These above results question such notions. In these results it appears as though the participants find it rather easy to distinguish between emotional and (conscious) cognitive experiences.

5.2.2 Somatic Experiences in Art Appreciation

"The body informs the logic of thinking about art", write Joy and Sherry (2003: 259). They base this statement upon their investigations of embodiment processes among the museum-going public. Also in their study, somatic experiences show themselves as important parts of experiences with art. Although the body, in a constant interaction with its environment, shapes thoughts and emotions (e.g.: Lakoff and Johnson 1999), the way in which such a process occurs remains unclear. This study of the relation between cognition and emotion as it appears in relation to art somewhat illuminates the role of the body in emotional and cognitive experiences.

Some participants have relatively strong somatic experiences in their meetings with art. In three of the interviews, the participants' somatic experiences are significant parts of both their affective and cognitive states. In one of the interviews, the participant's somatic experience influences her evaluation of the experience. A somatic marker for preference-making as proposed by Damasio and described in Chapter two, appears at the phenomenal level (1994, 1999, and 2003). Strong somatic experiences appear as a marker for decision-making and are incorporated in powerful emotional experiences.

An obvious example of somatic experiences in art appreciation is evident in Lise's description. She evaluates her experiences with art at least partly through her correlating physical and affective reactions. She rejects the creation *Meaning is What Hides the Instability of Ones Position* by Sanders and Geyer due, to some extent, to her unpleasant affects and bodily sensations. She states: "My experience was not a good one. My heart started to pound and I could notice that I started to become irritable". It is an experience wherein she appears to be frustrated and overpowered by the art work, and where she almost immediately wants to leave it. Her experience appears related to Schachter and Singer's theory of emotion, described in chapter three, wherein it may appear as though she experiences physiological arousal, then cognition (1962). She describes the experience as one where her physiological arousal with the cognitive label determines the nature of her affective experience. Her bodily and affective experiences serve as orienting principles for her interpretation of the art work.

In other experiences with art, Lise's bodily sensations can take on a very different form. For instance, she finds great pleasure in viewing trees, both in art works and in nature. One of her experiences of trees within art works produces a physical sensation that correlates with an experience of happiness. She senses a "bubble" in her chest, which she keeps referring back to and which she appears to use as a marker for the qualitative aspects of experience. It becomes evident that she uses her physical sensations as ways of making comparative judgments between experiences. In this case, she compares a different experience to the one above, stating that "it is still very different, because I did not have the same bubbly experience". She uses her somatic marker as a criterion for judging the quality of her experience. Moreover, within this interview, she only mentions a positive somatic marker as correlating with the experiences she ranks highest, and a negative one with the art work she rejects; her bodily experiences seems to be a marker for differing preferences.

Lise's strong bodily sensations appear related to relatively strong affective states and not to her experiences of a more cognitive nature. For instance, the final experience she describes seems to be a cognitive one that lacks the physical manifestation present in her previous experience. Here she experiences a kind of pleasure derived from a cognitive appreciation. She appreciates the whole exhibition for its resonance of historical creativity, greatness, and development. Such an experience seems to give her a framework for understanding one's historical inter-dependence and situated-ness. She describes a different kind of pleasure that is triggered by thoughts and which does not contain any particular physical sensations.

The use of metaphors is extant throughout her descriptions of her experience with art. Her choices of metaphors illuminate her bodily experience of emotions and, at least partly, her implicit views about emotions. For instance, she seems to regard happiness as an entity with a physical location. She states that the happiness she experiences when viewing a picture is located in her chest. She, thereby, uses an ontological metaphor wherein happiness is an entity that can be both identified and quantified (Lakoff and Johnson 1980). It is a primary metaphor as described by Lakoff and Johnson because the account of happiness as a physical entity is based upon its bodily grounding in her sensi-motoric experience (1999). Happiness, as the target for description, is given substance and structure through her bodily sensations. Along a similar line, she states that one can "perceive a bubble of happiness inside you", which substantiates the above interpretation of happiness experienced as a physical force. Additionally, it reflects basic notions of embodiment through the use of container schemata: the chest contains the happiness. The metaphor can also be elaborated through "conceptual blending". Happiness is a more abstract and complex concept partly explained by her concrete physical sensation that correlates with her subjective raw feel of happiness. Following Fauconnier and Turner's suggestion for conceptual blending, the bubble is the source domain and happiness is the target domain (2002). Looking in *Roget's Thesaurus of English Words and Phrases* the word "bubble" can be replaced by several first-order adjectives, including insubstantial thing, brief span, minuteness, lightness, flow and deception (2000). "Bubble" and "happiness", then, share a generic space wherein the bubble has a geometrical, physical shape that somewhat corresponds with the notion of happiness as a physical sensation. Here they also appear to share the characteristics of being elusive, temporary and ephemeral. The "Bubble of happiness" metaphor, then, appears in the blend to capture both physical and mental aspects of happiness. Happiness is experienced as consisting of components: it is succinct and translucent, with both directly physical aspects (sensations), but also containing a particular feel of experience. The blend from "bubble of happiness" creates a further, new blend as she states that "The sensation [of a bubble of happiness] is joined/kept together with the thoughts you have". It is a metaphorical use, whereby thoughts and physically-located sensations are connected in the blend. In such a blend, then, the experience of thoughts being of an embodied nature is explicitly revealed.

Another participant, Lars, also uses the bubble metaphor for happiness. Lars becomes happy when viewing several works by Asger Jorn (1914-1973), a Danish artist famous for his abstract impressionistic paintings. There is one particular painting by Jorn that is his favourite – "that gives him the most" – at the moment.

He becomes very happy by viewing the picture and describes the happiness this way: "It becomes just so, it bubbles like this when I see him". He states this as he is making a popping sound with his mouth. In addition to representing the happiness as a bubble, then, he regards it as analogous to the sound he makes. The use of the bubble as a somatic marker is not as direct in this case, as it has no direct reference to the bubble being of the body. Nevertheless, it can be regarded as a somatic marker through the blend of happiness, "bubble" and sound. Viewing the bubble as representing a real, geometrical shape, and viewing the sound he makes as also tangible in the moment of its making, the experience of happiness is partly explained as tangible, and may be regarded as a somatic marker as it correlates with his most favourable experience.

For a third participant, Kristina, her somatic experiences are also clearly present in her meeting with art. Even in the interview, she can feel a sensation that is a repetition of the one she has felt viewing an exhibit in Lisbon by Antony Gormley, a British artist who continuously sculptures the human form in various media and various contexts. Kristina contends that the sensation is located in the solar plexus. This sensation appears to be rather identical to the original sensation, and she says "I can really notice it in my stomach when I think about it [the exhibit]…I can notice it in the solar plexus…if I notice either discomfort or pleasure, it is here". As she says this, she touches her abdomen. Both happiness and discomfort, then, can correlate with such physical sensation in her stomach.

Kristina continues to describe art works that elicit discomfort in her, but when the nature of the exhibit radically changes, her bodily experiences also change and she experiences "lightness". It is an enormous relief and she feels reprieved. It is a release from her discomfort that alters her own sensations and affects. Her experience of nausea dissipates; the art work improves her condition radically. She has already seen this part of the exhibit once, but now it holds a very different meaning for her. This part now appears linked to the other parts and together these parts become a united work of art. The art work appears balanced and restores her sense of balance. She exemplifies how the museum forces certain movements that shape one's affects, and she views herself as having gone through a range of affects and bodily movements. Reflecting upon the experience, she contends that her body followed the nature of the bodies that were exhibited. She changes from feeling heavy, then questioning, then light and almost dissolved – the same characteristics that she perceives the art objects to contain.

In conclusion, it is evident from these interviews that the participants' experience of the body shapes their experience with art. Their somatic experiences also appear as part of their affective reactions; their bodily experience is an important aspect of their experience with art, and seems to be a part of, or at least correlates with, their affective experiences. Such body awareness is not always present, and if one proposes a continuum from emotional to cognitive experiences, the body appears highly apparent in their strong emotional experiences yet subtle to non-existent at the far end of the cognitive segment. However, the relationship between emotion, cognition and conscious somatic experiences becomes more complex by noting that Lise directly evaluates her experience with art, at least partly according to her physical sensation. Her evaluation seems to be a phenomenological manifestation of Damasio's somatic marker hypothesis, wherein her bodily sensations seem to be a significant factor for her evaluation of the experiences. This evaluation, however, is a reflective act. It appears, then, that a somatic marker may be involved more extensively in decision-making than Damasio proposed. He proposed unconscious and conscious somatic markers for the more automated, pre-reflective kinds of decision-making. Still, in this case, it is a somatic marker that she uses to evaluate the nature of her emotional experience.

5.2.3 Volitional Aspects of Emotions

Several of the participants view emotions as happening to them without their control. For instance, Lise was so disturbed by the art work that she contends she felt overpowered and in a highly unpleasant emotional state. Similarly, Siv considers affects to be involuntary, such that paintings can elicit emotions that she does not want to experience. These experiences are in accord with, for instance, the *OED*, which states that emotions are distinct from cognition and volition. Also, Ekman asserts that emotions are experienced as being involuntary reactions (see Chapter one). Lakoff as well as Zoltan Kövecses show anger metaphors that underscore anger as involuntary and outside of conscious control (Lakoff 1987; Kövecses 2000).

However, Lise also experiences emotions and bodily (physical) forces as powerful forces for action and motivation. As with all the participants, she places herself within the situations she wants to be. She visits museums where she can experience desired affective states. Likewise, at home she turns off the radio when such an action will remove unwanted affects. Siv chooses to view pictures that place her in a comfortable, contemplative state, and removes herself from pictures that she finds disturbing. It is evident, then, that emotions, to a certain extent, can be controlled through manipulation of one's environment. The folk-theory of emotions as passive (Zajonc 2000) appears persuasive in these interviews, but through this phenomenological investigation, it is obvious that the participants change their experience according to their desired emotional state. They spend time with art work that elicits the affective state they want to experience, and, conversely, remove themselves from situations that provoke undesired emotions.

Such behaviour questions the notions of emotions as being passive, animalistic impulses. Are emotions passive if it is one's act of will that moves one towards objects that elicits them? It also underscores the problem of differentiation and causality, considering emotions as being separated by their causes, as independent phenomena.

5.3 Classifications of Affect

Here an attempt is made to delineate a classification of the affective phenomena that includes results discussed in the first part. It also extracts new material from the interviews, and is supplemented and expanded upon by existing literature. It, therefore, departs from the phenomenological investigation and includes supplementary positions that may be used to support and enhance the classification.

The fundamental layers of the participants' emotional psyche have been investigated, and it is obvious that the participants encounter a variety of experiences that seem somewhat similar and which may be categorised as belonging to the same family of events. These experiences appear to be "emotion-like", i.e.: affective, and seem to take a plurality of forms. It, therefore, seems preferable to investigate the emotional phenomena and their alleged cognitive modulations in comparison with and in contrast to their bordering phenomena.

From the review of the neuropsychological, functional and phenomenal levels, as well as from the review of the literature on art appreciation, it is obvious that the relationships between cognition and the affective phenomena take a plurality of forms. These can be exemplified by the exploration of experiences with art. Within the psycho-physical tradition, the nature of pleasure has been questioned via the distinction between "pure sensation" and "unconscious cognition". In the cognitive tradition of art appreciation, the perspective that emotion is a by-product of conscious cognition is stressed. From the vantage point of emotional appreciation, emotional reactions are postulated as being immediate responses to expressive features, containing only unconscious cognition. It is somewhat similar to the aesthetic experience, wherein emotions are given a distinct form according to the existential dilemmas that elicit them. Here the cognition involved is also unconscious and the transition from unconscious cognition to emotion is the significant and vital mental process. In the psychoanalytic tradition, affects in relation to art appreciation may be results of cathartic effects, and as they are experienced, involve a deep sense of pleasure, related only to cognition in the sense that they elicited the feeling. In Kjørup's examinations of meetings with art, wherein feelings and cognition are interwoven, one major task of feelings is to direct attention. From the perspective of art appreciation as a hermeneutical endeavour, the role of feelings and emotions in self-understanding and meaning creation is an unresolved question. Therefore, in experiences with art, emotions and affects, as extant in various relationships with cognition, are revealed and explored.

The necessity of a distinguishing between affects that can comprise the variation in the affective experiences of the participants and the variations postulated within art appreciation is now stressed, and a delineation of the affective phenomena is in order, for only in such a context can the cognitive modulation of emotion be meaningfully placed. What follows, then, is an attempt at situating the affective concepts of psychology, based mainly upon the experiences of the participants. A nomenclature of the kind explicated here should be based upon the results of numerous studies, not just upon generalisations of the results obtained in the few interviews that have been conducted. What follows, then, is a revised taxonomy of the affective phenomena, based upon the results of the phenomenological investigation set against research from various areas that also seek to illuminate the issues. The taxonomy is, therefore, a result of a phenomenological investigation, supplemented by theoretical and empirical studies by other researchers.

5.3.1 Affect

As stated above, the participants experience a variety of phenomena that have the nature of what frequently are classified as "affects". They experience what may be characterised as moods, emotions and feelings. An attempt is made to delineate the nature of these experiences in the following nomenclature. Since the participants experience a variety of somewhat similar-looking phenomena that are somewhat difficult to distinguish between, it becomes clear that a common term should be used to encircle them. "Affections", or "affect", can continue to be used as an umbrella term, and can be subdivided into the phenomena of emotions, mood and feelings.

According to Max Bennett and Peter Hacker, a contemporary neuroscientist and a philosopher, respectively, these affective phenomena gradate into the phenomena of attitudes which include like/dislike evaluations as well as into endorsements and rejections (2003). Moreover, they contend that the affective phenomena parse into more stable features, or character traits, such as compassion, irritability or malevolence (ibid.). Based upon the participants' experiences, it is difficult to perceive any sharp distinctions between what are now called affective phenomena and these latter two categories of character traits and like-dislike evaluations. Theoretically, there are currently no clear criteria upon which to base inclusions and exclusions of phenomena, and it may be that these latter two categories exist in an overlapping grey area between affects and other mental states.

5.3.2 Mood

As mentioned in the findings section, Lise experiences a state wherein she is disturbed and ill at ease. It is, at first, a very intense experience and its effects last for several hours. It had been agreed that she was going to be interviewed after she had seen the exhibit, but she felt too disturbed to communicate. The interview was, therefore, conducted two days afterwards. A similar, long-lasting state is reported by Siv as she can feel contemplative and relaxed for extended periods of time when she views certain pictures. It appears as a calm experience that can last for relatively long periods.

It seems possible to distinguish between Lise's early reaction and its later descriptions. Lise's later affective reaction seems somewhat similar to Siv's experience, as both can be extended in time and remain fairly constant, without significant peaks. These experiences appear as what one may be able to classify as moods.

Within the literature, there seems to be some general acceptance that moods are states of mind that involve a "proneness to feel" (Bennett and Hacker 2003: 302). The temporal existence of moods can be of various durations, lasting for a couple of hours up to several months. For instance, Bennett and Hacker claim that a mood can be relatively brief (not as brief as an emotion), but also involve "longer term dispositional states" (ibid.: 302). One may, for example, "be depressed, melancholic, joyful, jovial, irritable or cheerful for an afternoon, or one may be suffering from a long-term depression that lasts for months" (ibid.: 302). Moods lack the same object-directedness that emotions have and, therefore, can be said to be of a different intentional quality. Moreover, moods differ from emotions in their causes and consequences. The causes of one's moods may appear oblique and impenetrable, and do not necessarily motivate for action. Rather, they colours one's existence at the time of their being until another affective state, or a different state of consciousness, takes over.

5.3.3 Emotions

There are many examples of the participants experiencing what may be classified as emotions. Therese, for instance, experiences several in her meetings with art. At the current visit she experiences disappointment in regards to the exhibition, *Meaning is What Hides the Instability of Ones Position*, by Sanders and Geyer, and she decides not to spend any significant time with it. She identifies cause(s) of her disappointment relatively easily. She has previously seen works by one of the artists and found these to be very funny. She expected to find this creation funny, but her anticipation was not met. The disappointment is of a relatively brief duration, and vanishes when she views other exhibits at the museum. Conversely, Therese frequently becomes happy when she views art, she contends. It does not need to be a pretty picture that elicits the happiness. It can be elicited by the awareness of the fact that someone actually made the art work; that they care to communicate their experiences. Here, then, the experience also has a rather direct relationship to an object. It is mainly caused by evaluations of the nature of art and its relationship to what she calls "important aspects of existence".

Lars also experiences what may be regarded as emotions. He becomes irritated when viewing *Meaning is What Hides the Instability of Ones Position* by Sanders and Geyer, the same exhibition with which Therese experiences disappointment. The irritation remains present throughout the time he spends with the art work. He connects the irritation with a lack of control over the art work, and the irritation dissipates soon after he leaves it. Differently, he becomes happy when viewing several works by Asger Jorn. At this point, it is the Asger Jorn one that gives him "the most". Before viewing his favourite picture by Jorn, he becomes aware of its close proximity and experiences what he calls "the happiness of anticipation". When he views the picture, he appears to have accompanying somatic experiences as discussed earlier.

Kristina experiences what she names as fear in response to an exhibit by Antony Gormley that she has previously viewed. A part of the exhibit elicits fright associated with images of systematised terror within her. She finds this part of the exhibit to exude a sinister and dismal atmosphere. Had it not been for the presence of other people, she would have left immediately. It was no particular object that created the fear, but the entire atmosphere. As she enters into other areas of the exhibit, she anticipates frightening works. Still, when the nature of the exhibit changes her frightened state dissipates. She experiences a release from her discomfort; her sensations and affects are altered. Her accompanying experience of nausea dissipates and the art work improves her condition radically.

The above descriptions are comprised of several similar features. The descriptions are alike in that they are of relatively brief duration, their immediate causes can be identified, and the experiences appear as important peaks in the participants' narratives. In Kristina's account, it is especially clear that a "feeling" component is present. During her fear reaction, Kristina experiences a strong "feel" constituted with a particular bodily location. Later, this "feel" acquires a different character, changing as the exhibit changes. Her experience, then, most closely approximates the theoretical characterisation of emotions in Chapter one.

The above psychological-phenomenological accounts are supported by the mainly theoretical delineation arrived at in Chapter one, where the conclusion was reached that emotions consist of various, causally-related components. This conclusion can now be expanded upon, and emotions can be viewed as consisting of spatial-temporal junctions, and from this collection of parts, a unified experience emerges. There exist numerous broad, prototypical kinds of emotions, and differences between these categories can be identified according to the interplay of their constituent parts. The various emotions can be differentiated according to their cognitive content, their subjective feel, their physiology, and their causes and consequences. To decide upon the inclusion and exclusion of the features in each particular emotion seems difficult since, again, there are no sound criteria upon which to base such a verdict. Phenomenological investigations can reveal descriptions of conscious emotional experience, wherefrom a further differentiation of components can continue.

Although it may be premature to name the necessary component parts of emotions, they do seem to always include a cognitive component. As Lazarus argues, emotions are always responses to meaning, and to paraphrase Zajonc, emotions are about the self in relation to objects[1] (1980: 157). The cognitive components

---

[1] Zajonc uses the word *affective* reactions and states that affective reactions are always in relation to the self and often about the self in relation to objects.

can, therefore, be understood as a feature that aids in the differentiation between the various emotions. Cognition appears easier to discern and characterise, especially when contrasted with subjective, feeling elements. Emotions, then, are directed toward an object or objects and are expressions of and encouragements of activity.

Emotions and conscious cognition can be experienced as clearly separable. The distinction between cognitive and emotional experiences may be caused by the sensations and feelings involved in emotions which cognition seem to lack (although Damasio would argue differently). Emotions may, however, be adjusted and refined by both conscious and unconscious cognition; they may be in a state of continuous change according to a concurrent and continuous evaluation of stimuli. The cognition involved may also be a reaction to the emotional experience itself. The notion of emotions being of an involuntary nature may be partly explained by the involvement of unconscious cognition. Obviously, emotions cannot be fully measured through skin conductance responses as such measurements only indirectly assess the sensations, or maybe the feelings, that are a part of the emotion. A question for further research may concern the nature of cognition involved in affects and emotions. Cognition is not a unitary phenomenon, and to delineate its involvement in emotion is a complex task.

The meaning of an emotion arises from the particular individual's experience, including the cultural context. Individual differences in emotion appear impossible to currently assess, and as Funch contends, there appear to be infinite possibilities of variation within emotional experiences (1997). Bergson presented such a line of thought and argued that emotions, such as happiness and grief, do not exist as quantitative gradations, but are qualitatively different (1888/1980). For instance, in everyday linguistic practices one says that one is "very happy" or "not so happy" and, thereby, accords happiness a mathematical relationship wherein one is larger than the other, and where the former state also contains the latter. Bergson showed that when we do this it is because we deal with emotions pragmatically and avoid "the deeper" emotions. He showed that emotions have qualitatively different characteristics according to their intensities, describing what one regards as different intensities of the same emotion. Moreover, he argued that these qualitatively different emotions have merging transitions, meaning that states of consciousness cannot be viewed as separate states extended in time, but, rather, have to be viewed as containing all previous states and, also, as anticipating future ones. It is an unceasing fusion of experience. An emotion, then, is never identical to a previous one, and is a collection of all previous experiences that, at the same, time anticipate future experiences. Therefore, by referring to prototypical experiences, the rich nuances of emotional life may be lost, yet this referencing facilitates for communication of meaning, however crude or pragmatic.

5.3.4 Feelings

Earlier on in this chapter "feelings" were expanded upon in relation to somatic experiences. To further substantiate feelings based upon the participants' accounts may not be supportable from the current data. Thus, what follows is an attempt to describe feelings in a theoretical fashion.

Feelings appear to be different from emotions. As emphasised in Chapter one, emotions are more labyrinthine and more theory-filled while feelings appear basic and less differentiated. They appear as a universal human property (Wierzbicka 1994). Emotions may contain feelings, but this relationship is not bi-directional. In other words, feelings do not contain emotions. Throughout this essay it has become apparent, however, that feelings are of various kinds and causes. What follows is an attempt at explicating various kinds of feelings.

Several kinds of feelings arise from the senses. According to Dan Zahavi, Husserl makes it clear that one should differentiate between two modes of sensing (2001: 146, 158). One the one hand, there is an experience of the body's position and movements (the kinaesthetic); it is a kind of bodily "self-consciousness". On the other hand, there is sense content, which refers to visual or tactile sense impressions of, for example, "pain, lust, nausea etc" (ibid.: 90). These latter kinds of sense impressions are given meaning, or are "meaningfully configured", according to the body's continually positioning (ibid.: 91). There exists kinaesthetic sensing, then, that appears related to the way the body in general is perceived, and this sensing or feeling may be related to Merleau-Ponty's description of the body where feelings may appear as a "general sensibility of the body". They are pre-reflective states, but, as such, can be reflected upon. Then there are the visual and tactile sense impressions.

Similar to the visual and tactile sense impressions are what Bennett and Hacker categorise as feelings that are appetites, such as "hunger, thirst and lust" (2003). According to Bennett and Hacker, the appetites consist of a mix of sensations and desires that are typical of animals. Such desires are characterised according to their object proper, in that they have rather specific associated objects; thirst, for example, slaked by fluid intake. These appear to be phenomena that are closer to brute impulses. Yet, the extent to which cognition is involved in experiences of appetites may be investigated, as in meditative practices where one may attempt to, at least partly, have power over the subjective experience of the appetites. Then there is a different category that appears closely related to the appetites, yet still distinguished from them as their antecedents and consequences are of different natures. This category includes awareness of feelings such as "tiredness, lassitude or fatigue" (ibid.: 200).

There appear, then, to be several different kinds of feelings. Visual and tactile sensations are one kind, clearly of bodily origin and with an apparent external reference. There are also the kinaesthetic sensations that also are strongly linked to the body and which seem to involve feeling as a form of internal awareness of body positioning. A third kind of sensation, or feeling, can be such sensations as some of the participants were experiencing, including a "bubble in the chest", and a "sensation in the solar plexus". This third kind seems distinct from the first two, and may involve particularly engrained cognition. Kövecses argues, for instance, that certain feelings/sensations are, in part, culturally resolute (2000). According to Taylor and Mbeuse, Zulus experience a "squashing in the heart" in the beginning stage of anger (1998; cited in Kövecses 2000: 187). Matsuki states that, for the Japanese, intense anger "(…) comes to the head with a 'click'" 1995; cited in Kövecses 2000: 187). It may be that individuals in these respective cultures are the only ones to experience such sensations. Such sensations or feelings may, therefore, have cognitive (conscious or unconscious) components that are culturally distinct.

Additionally, there may be a fourth kind: a "feel of experience" that includes the above kinds. This "feel of experience" has frequently been named qualia and comprises the qualitative properties of experience; the sensed or raw feels of mental states. By and large, they can be said to be "what it is like" to have a mental state. Qualia are "what it is like to be something", as detailed in Thomas Nagel's famous essay, *What Is It Like to Be a Bat?* (1974). Many philosophers wish to disclaim qualia, and maintain that qualia can be reduced to, as well as explained through, functional or physical accounts of the mind. Qualia are, however, one of the major problems for contemporary physicalist and functionalist accounts, as they currently are unable to fully explain the felt aspect of experience. Qualia are different from feelings, however. Feelings seem to include only those parts of experience that can be concretely "felt", and do not necessarily, in converse to qualia, include the experience of seeing a colour, i.e.: visual sensations. "Qualia" and "feeling" may be separate, but overlapping terms, or maybe feelings are sub-phenomena of qualia. Both feelings and qualia appear as ends in themselves, without being directed toward an external object.

One aspect of affective experience that is not fully included in the above descriptions is the possibility that experience may consist of a continuous feel – an affective tone that colours experience in a constant process. Conscious existence may have a continuous affective ambiance. Such kinds of feel may be without conscious cognition, and may be present among the continuous fluctuation of affective experiences. It appears irrefutable that many mental states have a property of a feeling, but it is certainly controversial to claim that all conscious mental experiences, including desires and beliefs, contain a felt aspect. Nevertheless, what follows is an attempt to argue for such.

One argument for a ceaseless feel can be found in the conception of "flow". As mentioned earlier in Chapter four, it has been argued that flow-experiences may improve one's quality of life, and contribute to overall contentment. The more frequently a person experiences flow, the happier the person is. A flow experience, however, is a state one is only aware of in retrospect. In "flow" one is absorbed in an activity to the extent that there is a loss of ego, an unawareness of one's own identity. The sense of self is dissolved in the experience, and it involves an upheaval of subject/object distinctions. Thus, when one experiences flow, one is not aware of one's own affects and emotions, yet afterwards the experience is regarded as a highly pleasurable. Therefore, although one is not always aware of the current affective state, one can reflect upon it and give it an affective description.

To continue the argument, there is no such thing as a neutral state of consciousness, as it will always involve an awareness of one's body positioning, as well as maybe this "feel" of experience. Moreover, a "neutral" state may be viewed in hindsight as an affective one that can be characterised as pleasurable: although water appears to be without taste, it is pleasurable to drink it, and even though unpolluted air may seem to have no odour, it has a whiff that is pleasant. In the case of "cold cognition", i.e. cognition without apparent emotions, they can, in a reflective act, be evaluated according to their hedonic tone. A cold cognition may also be considered a comfortable one. Conclusively, it may be, then, that experience consists of, among its other features, a constant oscillation between various affective states, i.e.: the individual is always in one affective state or another. In this most "basic" of feelings, it may be that there is close to a complete separation between conscious cognition and emotion, and the degree of perception involved in the emotion may be relatively minimal. It is, however, in a retrospective, cognitive act that such feeling is discovered, thus, the intertwined aspects of cognition and feeling persist.

Chapter 6
Discussion

6.1 Discussion of Findings

Some significant findings arose from the analyses of people's experiences with art which illuminate the relationship between cognition and emotion. These are: that emotions may be experienced as devoid of conscious cognition; that there may exist a somatic marker for strong emotions that may also serve as a marker for a retrospective evaluation of the experience; and that to experience an emotion may partly be an act of volition.

6.1.1 Emotion without Conscious Cognition

The assertion that emotion may be experienced as devoid of conscious cognition is currently somewhat controversial. As mentioned earlier, both Zajonc and Lazarus claim that, "in nature", cognition and emotion are fused and inseparable. Zajonc extends his claim further than Lazarus does, as he views cognition as conscious. In this investigation, several of the participants' descriptions contain distinctions between cognition and emotion, and such observations are accentuated by their use of metaphors, as seen in the previous chapter. That emotion is experienced as devoid of conscious cognition does not mean, however, that no cognition is involved as it is evident that unconscious cognition is a robust phenomenon.

Support for such differentiation between conscious and unconscious cognition can be found in the reviewed literature. Although Zajonc's experimental evidence seems confounded, he develops a line of reasoning containing several sound arguments as to why affect and (conscious) cognition should be viewed as distinct, and why affective states are constant features of experience while cognition is not. The following are some of the most powerful arguments from this line of thought.

In an interpersonal encounter, what one most clearly remembers is not the objective features of the person, but one's own emotional reactions to them; the ambiance of a situation can be remembered more clearly than its particular content. Any interpersonal meeting consists of constant variations of seemingly affective reactions, such as attraction or repulsion. Emotion permeates social interaction, and is a main feature for the exchange of meaning. For example, Michael Argyle et al. studied the consequences of statements uttered in various tones of voice and found that the interpretations of the statements were heavily influenced by the tone (1970). Research into how impressions are formed shows that affective reactions are strong and persuasive, such that the affective evaluation frequently remains, even in the case where the cognitive foundation for the affective reaction has been negated (Zajonc 1980: 157). Similarly, research on how attitudes are formed and sustained demonstrates that those having an affective aspect are resistant to change, even when cognitive information is given that should lead to a re-evaluation of the attitude. Emotional expressions can be decoded reliably, although the content of the statement has been denuded (Zajonc 1980). Paivio found that pleasant/unpleasant ratings came faster for images than for words (1978; cited in Zajonc 1980), which Zajonc concludes occurs because in images an affective reaction is immediately evaluated. Moreover, Zajonc argues that affects can occur at any point in a cognitive process, and he concludes that "affect is always present in thought whereas the converse is not true for cognition" (1980: 154).

This finding, then, of cognition and emotion being experienced as distinct, shows that there are differences between emotional and cognitive phenomena, emphasising that they may indeed be separate, but overlapping. Moreover, it underscores that cognition may be experienced in a variety of ways, that there exists a variety to cognitive phenomena (e.g.: conscious and unconscious), and that diverse kinds of cognition may be involved in emotion. It also stresses that conscious cognition is not constantly experienced; that it is possible, at a phenomenal level, to map, delineate and demarcate various affective and cognitive experiences as they come to pass. It seems possible, then, to distinguish between at least certain kinds of conscious emotional and conscious cognitive experiences. From such a differentiation, it follows that it may be inaccurate to use the broad term "understanding" to capture all kinds of meaningful experience, including all kinds of affective experience. Although the experience of an emotion contains unconscious cognition, it can be differentiated from conscious cognitive experiences. "Understanding" appears to be a term of decisive cognitive content, and its inclusion of affective phenomena seems uncertain. As delineated in Chapter four, Gadamer uses the term "understanding" to denote consequences of meaning-creating events. "Understanding" captures the way he views experience as occuring: as a mental oscillation between observing the parts and the whole. Arguably, emotions form meaning-creating experiences, and if such events occur in a hermeneutic circle, then an affective term should be explicitly included. Lakoff and Johnson's cognitive model for experience may also, for the same reason, be somewhat imprecise.

6.1.2 Somatic Experiences in Emotion

In regards to the somatic marker, the term is mainly applied to sensations that accompany cognition as a tool for decision-making. Feelings and sensations have frequently been claimed as accompanying emotions, although there exist cognitive stances wherein it is thought that sensations or feelings are considered as unnecessary for the experience of an emotion. In these interviews it becomes clear that feelings or sensations are pronounced in the participants' relatively "strong" emotional experiences, and it is possible that sensations or feelings take on a different form for "milder" emotional experiences. If there indeed are somatic markers both for emotions and cognition, the distinction between these two phenomena becomes more blurred. In the interview with Lise, however, it was through a retrospective evaluation of an affective experience that the somatic marker was used as a tool for decision-making. Hence, Damasio's somatic marker hypothesis is not necessarily supported by these findings. The nature of sensations in emotion and cognition are still unresolved, yet in these interviews, sensations occurred in experiences that were primarily characterised as emotion-laden.

6.1.3 Volitional Aspects

The third and final finding obtained from the interviews is that the experience of an emotion can be, at least partly, an act of will. The passivity of emotions has been stressed numerous times, yet the participants move and remove themselves in relation to objects that elicit emotions and moods. They approach objects or situations that bring forth desired affective states and withdraw from those that extract unwanted states. The notion of emotions being at least partly volitional distances emotions further from being mere animalistic impulses. At the same time, it appears as though emotions cannot be fully experienced at will, as the participants also stress how they experience emotions to be overpowering. Therefore, it may be that once an emotion is experienced, both conscious and unconscious appraisals and other evaluations can adjust it and give it shape. Consequently, the notion that emotion is an animalistic impulse, or in the converse, suffused with reason, may present too strong a dichotomy. The truth may lie somewhere in the middle. A different interpretation could be that emotions are of such heterogeneous kinds that they may extend to polar ends of such an experiential continuum.

A similar consequence of the assertion that emotions are volitional is that Sartre's distinction between false and genuine emotions becomes too strong a differentiation between the two. As stated in Chapter three, according to Sartre, a genuine emotion is one wherein one has no choice in the matter; the emotion is experienced as a powerful and involuntary response. A false emotion, then, is a product of one's volitional attempt to experience it. If the account of emotions arrived at in Chapter one proves itself to be the most plausible, such differentiation between genuine and false emotion would be confounded. Emotions contain both active and passive aspects.

The conclusion that emotions are partly volitional is based upon the clarification of emotions arrived at in Chapter one, wherein emotions are said to be composed of various, casually-related components, including both their causes and consequences. One apparent problem that arises from such a position, however, is that it rejects a certain stance on causality. According to Reisenzein and Schönpflug, it has, since the work of the influential 17th century Scottish philosopher David Hume, been generally accepted that causes and consequences must be distinct, singular events (1992: 37). Only by viewing causality this way does one avoid the possibility of self causation: that an event results in itself. However, MacDonald and MacDonald underscore that per David Marr and Donald Davidson, respectively a leading 20th century psychologist and philosopher, it has become clear that one can distinguish between levels of explanation and description, and that such distinction can confound Hume's view (1995). It is not, then, necessarily incompatible with current accounts of causality to view emotions as constituted by its causes and effects.

6.2 Methodological Reflections

Within the qualitative tradition, numerous criteria have been proposed for evaluating quality. Since one of Kvale's proposed means of investigation has been used, his methods for evaluating the quality of the research will be applied (1997).

Kvale contends that quality and validity originate in the harmony and accord extant in the particular research process (ibid.). This means that there is a correspondence between the theme one investigates and the participants one chooses, that the process of analysis is logical and springs from the nature of the material, and that the researcher places emphasis on that which is central in the participants' stories in conjunction with the theme of the research. The research process should also be clearly documented and communicated, so that the reader can evaluate the validity of the study; it should be a transparent course of investigation. Additionally, Kvale recommends that the whole study should be evaluated in accord with the validity criteria that are relevant to the respective study, and that it is made clear in which context the research conclusions are relevant. Overall, validity is dependent upon the quality of the "craftsmanship" of the research process in its entirety. One way quality can be provided for, then, is through investigations into sources of "in-quality". What follows is a discussion of certain potential weaknesses of quality within this project.

6.2.1 Issues of Particularity

One main critique is that the results obtained may be too particular. They may be a result of the particular researcher's interpretations and the descriptions given by the specific participants. This is a common critique of qualitative methods, which are primary tools for the humanities and social sciences, yet have frequently been criticised for yielding results that are too subjective and particular. Rasmus Helles and Simo Køppe as well as Kennedy note that if research findings do not extend beyond their own immediacy or particularity toward some general concerns, then the theoretical as well as practical applicability will be rather limited and restricted (Helles and Køppe 1999; Kennedy 1979). Helles and Køppe also note, however, that no phenomenon is completely unique, not even a work of art (ibid.).

Can one reach a strong conclusion, then, that is valid for more than the particular circumstances, based on results from qualitative methods, frequently involving only a few participants? A few points are worth mentioning. Strong conclusions have been attained based upon case-histories; they have historical precedence in that some of the most famous psychological theories have been based on case-histories. Continuing this trend, contemporary clinical and neuropsychological findings are frequently based on single case studies. On a more theoretical note, ways of generalising from small samples continue as a mode of inquiry, and Kvale discusses various ways of making generalisations (1997). He claims that in qualitative methods analytical generalisation is particularly important, whereby a study is evaluated both for its particularity as well as for what appears common to other research. As long as contextual information is given and the research process is relatively transparent, then researchers of other projects can evaluate and relate the results to their own particular work.

In this case, the findings from this qualitative study have been compared and supported by existing theory, thereby furthering the likelihood of a valid conclusion.

6.2.2 Issues of Language and First-Person Perspective
There are, however, other problems that may confound the research, one being any linguistic issues involved in interpreting and translating interview results from Danish into English. It may be that the transfer of meaning is inaccurate and that certain finer linguistic distinctions are lost. The conclusions reached, nevertheless, are not necessarily dependent upon the particular, fine language.

The participants' accounts have been viewed as factual and representative of their experiences. However, there are obstacles to having such confidence in the interview material, as subjective experiences are only fully available to the participant who has the experience. To be fully accurate about the participants' experiences is most likely impossible for the obvious reason that they are individual accounts, occurring at a first-person perspective. There is no immediate access to their experiences, and as soon as the interviews are completed, there are no continuous "negations of meaning" and no feedback on the intentions behind the participants' statements (Fairclough 2003). An extended negotiation of the results could have been conducted by asking the participants for their evaluation of the interpretations. Such validation, however, is not unproblematic (see e.g. Fog 1992 for an explication of potential problems).

There are no indications of the participants' accounts being unreliable, and it appears as though all the participants made genuine attempts to communicate their experiences. Their accounts also appeared independent, in that they were not shaped to fit the interviewer's expectations. In the interviews, the participants all attempted to clarify, adjust and correct the interpretations of their statements. However, as Chalmers underscores, methodologies for investigating first-person data may still be in its infancy (2004). The aspiration, however, is not to reach a perfect account of the experience of emotion and cognition, but simply to reach an improved characterisation (adjusted from Chalmers 2004), and through the newer methods of qualitative research, some of the difficulties of "private experiences" are circumvented.

This book has attempted to uncover subtle aspects of experience. Especially in relation to emotion, there seems to exist a linguistic inadequacy, such that it is difficult, or maybe impossible, to fully communicate one's experiences. One indication of this linguistic gap is the quantity of exclamations in these interviews, as the participants frequently uttered statements such as "It was wonderful", without being further able to describe the experience. There seems to be a verbal deficiency in the illustrations of feelings.

In regards to the interpretation of metaphors, there is at least one noteworthy point. Joseph and Roberts cite the work of Norris and eloquently put forth that maybe "it is impossible to reduce truth, without remainder, to the endless play of metaphorical displacement" (Joseph and Roberts 2004: 16; Norris 2004). For instance, as will be argued in the next section, it may be that emotional experience is direct, immediate and, thus, impossible to fully capture via the cognitive-linguistic model for the nature of metaphors which has been used here. However, as Joy and Sherry explain, through such analysis of metaphors, one can reveal structures of the cognitive unconscious (2003). The analysis of metaphors and the condensation of meaning appeared in this investigation as complimentary processes of analysis. In meaning condensation the material is being compressed, i.e.: the material is being "closed down", giving a proper overview of the material. In the analysis of metaphors, the material is being "opened

up" and given the possibility for continuous analysis and interpretation.

6.2.3 Incommensurability?
Henning Olsen has reviewed Danish qualitative studies, and gives
several criteria by which qualitative analysis can be evaluated (2002,
see p. 148 for a summary). He points out that the investigation should
be thematically, methodologically, analytically and scientifically
coherent. A critique of the study reported in Chapter five could be that
it is not methodologically and scientifically coherent, as this book
assumes that these different levels of investigation can be coherently
compared and contrasted. In contrast to such an assumption, however,
it has been argued that theories of different paradigms[1] cannot be
understood externally – they are "incommensurable". No sound
evaluation between paradigms is possible, because the meanings of
their concepts and classifications will vary and are deeply ingrained in
the tradition's implicit assumptions. Accordingly, research paradigms
are impenetrable from the exterior, and only a researcher within the
paradigm can comprehend it. Accordingly, one cannot convert or
transform the results and assertions of one paradigm into another
(from Bem and Jong 1997). In this book, the theories at the differing
levels of concern as discussed in Chapter three can be said to represent
deviating paradigms; they may (but not necessarily) represent
differences in metaphysics. According to the incommensurability
principle, then, the investigation that has been conducted throughout
this book is not valid. However, the incommensurability stance has
been criticized by various realist positions for being relativistic.
Researchers holding such a position contend that there is an ordered
reality upon which research is based which allows for comparisons
between paradigms. Without such a reality, there would be no
explanation for the growth and success of science (Norris 2004).
Without diving deeper into the debate here, it is sufficient to note that
this book carries some underlying assumptions that are closer to a
realist position. Moreover, it is a book of high modernity, wherein it is
believed possible to create some order amidst the disunity. It is an
attempt to create understanding beyond "local occurrences".

---

[1] Within a paradigm a conceptual framework is implicitly and explicitly adhered to,
which includes an allegedly unified set of fundamental assumptions, a specified
methodology as well as the use of the similar instruments (Bem and Jong 1997).

6.2.4 What is Art?

The historically contentious question "What is art?" is too extensive to discuss or attempt to answer here. In order to avoid the question this study involved objects commonly accepted as art, that is, objects included in museums. Such a solution is, of course, not completely satisfactory, but seemed to be the only plausible way for this investigation to continue. To begin down the descriptive path of what art is would deserve minimally a whole book in its own right. Unfortunately, the solution in this project does not consider experiences with art within the communities, including art which rejects the museum as its place for presentation. This investigation has also been limited to discussing cognition in emotion in relation to experiences of artistic pictures within the realm of Western Art. It has been limited to include only adults, and did not include research into the phenomena as it develops in children, thereby bypassing the complex discussion of the beginning and development of cognition and emotion. Although such delineation would have been highly informative, a whole new, complex line of evidence would need to be reviewed and is beyond the scope of this book.

6.2.5 "Normal" Emotions

Emotion has also been discussed as a wide category or phenomenon and no single emotion has been specifically investigated. This has been an account of "normal" emotions, not of those that appear in pathological cases. Various levels of the human psyche from which the role of cognition in emotion has been outlined while different contemporary views on the ramifications of qualitative inquiry such as hermeneutics have only briefly been touched upon.

6.3 Conclusion

In conclusion, based upon a psychological-phenomenological investigation and theoretical considerations, the concepts "affect", "emotion", "mood", "feeling" and "cognition" carry definitive, discriminate meanings. Moods do not have the same object-directedness, or cognitive specificity, that emotions have. Emotions comprise a variety of different cognitions that can be of both an unconscious and conscious nature. In feelings, the cognition appears unconscious and seems to be of a very different kind than those apparent in emotions. Feelings appear largely as non-cognitive, while emotions will always have a cognitive component. These affective phenomena can be distinguished from cognition in that they have a qualitatively different "feel" from cognition. However, any strong dichotomies appear unwarranted, because, to paraphrase James' eloquence, they appear to "shade imperceptible into each other".

These different terms refer to various parts of experience and describe distinguishable, yet overlapping phenomena. By distinguishing between these affective phenomena, several of the contemporary debates may be resolved. Zajonc's experimental studies on like/dislike evaluations are not studies on emotion. It is even ambiguous whether a like/dislike evaluation should be contained within the affective category at all. Lazarus and Zajonc write about very different affective phenomena, wherein Lazarus discussed emotions which involve both conscious and subconscious cognition. Zajonc discusses like/dislike evaluations which may involve only subconscious cognition. Moreover, what Zajonc calls free-floating anxiety is described in such a way that it appears to be more of a mood than an emotion. Damasio investigates neural correlates of sensations, and part of LeDoux's research seems to focus upon reflexes. The sub-cortical route involves no cognition, and is not an emotion. Without diving deeply into Panksepp's studies, it seems as though he investigates a primary response system that does not involve emotions. The newer cognitive models of emotion appear to portray moods, emotions and primitive response systems, and should indicate such. Due to the controversies surrounding emotions, when discussing any account that contains affective phenomena, the nature of the affective phenomena needs to be explicitly delineated.

This book began with the words of William James, and through him, the study of emotion briefly moved to the forefront of psychology. Now, after a long silence throughout most areas of psychological research, emotions are again a central topic of investigation. James' way of conceptualising emotions lies at the heart of few contemporary emotion theories, and, according to the above taxonomy, what he considered to be full-blown emotion should be regarded rather as sense experience. Historical deviations in the use of concepts are not surprising. What has been made clear throughout this book, however, is that there exists a contemporary divergence in the use of affective terms, and that these variances confound attempts at investigating the nature of emotion. It is clear that conceptual clarifications are essential in order to initiate a more coherent research thrust. The development of terminology may come from, but is not necessarily limited to phenomenological-psychology as well as from the rules and logic of philosophy. A more coherent and improved emotion discourses will emerge from such ventures. Facilitating for greater discourse across the subfields of psychology will aid in the essential task of forestalling the continuing fragmentation within contemporary psychology. This book has been an initial attempt to meet this need.

Bibliography

Adamos, Maria M. 2002. 'How are the Cognitive and Non-cognitive Aspects of Emotions Related?' in *Consciousness and Emotion.* 3(2): 183-195.

Adolph, Ralph and Damasio, Antonio 2001. 'The Interaction of Affect and Cognition: a Neurobiological Perspective' in Forgas, J. P. (ed.) *Handbook of Affect and Social Cognition.* Mahwah: Lawrence Erlbaum Associates: 27-45.

Antonelli, Aldo G. 1998. 'Definition' in Craig, Edward (general ed.) *Routledge Encyclopedia of Philosophy.* Version 1.0. Routledge.

Argyle, M, Salter, V., Nicholson, H., Williams, M. and Burgess, P. 1970. 'The Communication of Inferior and Superior Attitudes by Verbal and Non-verbal Signals' in *British Journal of Social and Clinical Psychology.* 9:222-231.

Aristotle. 1984. *The Rhetoric and Poetic.* New York: The Modern Library. 367-347 or 335-322BC

Arnheim, Rudolf. 1974. *Art and Visual Perception: A Psychology of the Creative Eye. The New Version.* Berkeley: University of California Press.

Bechara, A., Damasio, H. and Damasio, A. 2000. 'Emotions, Decision-making and the Orbitofrontal Cortex' in *Cerebral Cortex.* 10: 295-307.

Bell, Clive. 1961. *Art.* London: Arrow Books. 1913

Bem, Sacha and Jong, Huib Looren de. 1997. *Theoretical Issues in Psychology. An Introduction.* London: Sage publications.

Bennett, M. R. and Hacker, P.M.S. 2003. *Philosophical Foundations of Neuroscience.* Oxford: Blackwell Publishing.

Ben-Ze'ev, Aaron. 2000. *The Subtlety of Emotions.* Cambridge, MA: The MIT Press

--. 2002. 'Emotions are not Feelings' in *Consciousness and Emotion* 3(1): 81-89.

Bergson, Henri. 1888/1980. *Det Uumiddelbare i Bevidstheden.* Vinten Forlag.

Bernasconi, Robert. 1986. 'Editors Introduction' in Gadamer, Hans-Georg *The Relevance of the Beautiful and Other Essays.* Cambridge: Cambridge University Press.

Block, Ned. 1994. 'Qualia' in Guttenplan, S. (ed.) *A Companion to the Philosophy of Mind.* Oxford: Blackwell publishers: 518-520.

Bornstein, R. F. 1989. 'Exposure and Affect: Overview and Meta-analysis of Research, 1968-1987' in *Psychological Bulletin*. 106: 265-289.

Chalmers, David J. 1996. *The Conscious Mind. In Search of a Fundamental Theory*. Oxford: Oxford University Press.

Chalmers, David J. 2004. 'How can we Construct a Science of Consciousness?' in Gazzeniga, M. (ed) *The Cognitive Neurosciences III*. MIT Press.

Churchland, P.M. and Churchland, P.S. 1981. 'Functionalism, Qualia and Intentionality' in *Philosophical Topics*. 12:121-132.

Cornelius, Randolph R. 1996. *The Science of Emotion. Research and Tradition in the Psychology of Emotion*. New Jersey: Prentice Hall

Cosmides, Leda. Tooby, John. 2000. 'Evolutionary Psychology and the Emotions' in Lewis, M. and Haviland-Jones, J.M (eds.) *Handbook of Emotions*. NY: Guilford: 91-115.

--. 2006. 'Evolutionary Psychology, Moral Heuristics and the Law' in Gigerenzer, E. and Engel, C. (eds) *Heuristics and the Law*. MIT Press:181-212.

Crane, Tim. 2001. *Elements of Mind: an Introduction to the Philosophy of Mind*. Oxford University Press.

Csikszentmihalyi, Mihaly and Robinson, Rick E. 1990. *The Art of Seeing*. Los Angeles: J. Paul Getty Museum.

Csikszentmihalyi, Mihaly. 1992. *Flow. The Psychology of Happiness*. London: Random House Ltd.

--. 1997. *Finding Flow. The Psychology of Engagement with Everyday Life*. New York: Basic Books.

Damasio, Antonio R. 1994. *Decartes' Error. Emotion, Reason and the Human Brain*. New York: G. P. Putnam's Sons

--. 1999. *The Feeling of What Happens. The Body and Emotion in the Making of Consciousness*. Harvest Books

--. 2003. *Looking for Spinoza. Joy, Sorrow and the Feeling Brain*. Harvest Books

Darwin, Charles.1998. *The Expression of the Emotions in Man and Animals*. London: Harper Collins Publishers. 1872.

Davidson, Richard J. 2003. 'Seven Sins in the Study of Emotion: Correctives from Affective Neuroscience' in *Brain and Cognition*. 52(1): 129.132.

Davidson, Richard J., Scherer, Klaus R. and Goldsmith, Hill H. 2003. *Handbook of Affective Sciences.* Oxford: Oxford University Press

Dennett, Daniel C. 1991. *Consciousness Explained.* Boston: Little Brown.

Descombes, Vincent. 1980. *Modern French Philosophy.* Cambridge University Press.

DeSousa, R. 1987. *The Rationality of Emotions.* Cambridge, MA: MIT Press.

Dickie, George. 1974. *Art and the Aesthetic: An Institutional Analysis.* Cornell University Press

Dolan, R. J. 2002. 'Emotion, Cognition and Behaviour' in *Science* 298: 1191-1194.

Dunn B.D., Dalgleish T. and Lawrence, A.D. 2006. 'The Somatic Marker Hypothesis: a Critical Evaluation'in *Neuroscience and Biobehavioural Reviews* 2: 239-271

Ekman, Paul. 2003. *Emotions Revealed. Recognizing Faces and Feelings to Improve Communication and Emotional Life.* New York: Times Books.

Eysenck, Michael W. and Keane, Mark T. 2000. *Cognitive Psychology. A Student's Handbook.* East Sussex: Psychology Press Ltd.

Fairbairn, W.R.D. 1938. 'The Ultimate Basis of Aesthetic Experience' in *British Journal of Psychology.* 29: 167-181.

Fairclough, Norman. 2003. *Analysing Discourse. Textual Analysis for Social Research.* London and New York: Routeledge.

Fauconnier, Gilles and Turner, Mark. 2002. *The Way We Think. Conceptual Blending and the Minds Hidden Complexities.* New York: Basic Books.

Flack, William F. and Laird, James D. (eds). 1998. *Emotions in Psychopathology. Theory and Research.* New York: Oxford University Press.

Fodor, Jerry.1983. *The Modularity of Mind: an Essay on Faculty Psychology.* Cambridge, Mass.: MIT Press

--. 1998. *Concepts: Where Cognitive Science Went Wrong.* Oxford: Clarendon Press

--. 2000. *The Mind Doesn't Work That Way: the Scope and Limits of Computational Psychology.* Cambridge, Mass.: MIT Press

Fog, Jette. 1992. 'Den Moralske Grund i Det Kvalitative Forskningsintervju' in *Nordisk Psykologi,* 3: 212-229.

Forgas, Jospeh P. 2003. 'Affective Influences on Attitudes and Judgements' in Davidson, Scherer, and Goldsmith (eds). *Handbook of Affective Sciences*. Oxford: Oxford University Press: 596-618

Fortenbaugh, W.W. 1975. *Aristotle on Emotion*. New York: Harper & Row Publishers, Inc.

Freud, Sigmund.1961. *Beyond the Pleasure Principle*. The Standard Edition (vol. 18). London: The Hogarth Press. 1920

--. 1961. *The Ego and the Id*. The Standard Edition (vol. 19). London: The Hogarth Press. 1923-25

Funch, Bjarne S. 1997. *The Psychology of Art Appreciation*. Copenhagen: Museum Tusculanum Press.

--. 2000. 'Hvorfor ser vi på Billedkunst?' in *Nordisk Museologi*. 1: 87-96.

Gadamer, Hans-Georg. 1989. *Truth and Method*. New York: The Continuum Publishing Company. 1960.

--. 1986. *The Relevance of the Beautiful and other Essays*. Cambridge: Cambridge University Press. 1970.

Gade, Anders. 1997. *Hjerneprocesser: Kognition og Neurovitenskab*. København: Frydenlund Grafisk.

Gardner, Howard. 1985. *The Mind's New Science. A History of the Cognitive Revolution*. New York: Basic Books

Gazzeniga, Michael S. and LeDoux, Joseph. 1978. *The Integrated Mind*. New York: Plenum.

Gazzaniga M. S., Ivry R. B. and Mangun G. R. 2002. *Cognitive Neuroscience. The Biology of the Mind*. New York and London: W.W. Norton & Company

Giddens, Anthony. 1990. *Consequences of Modernity*. Polity Press.

Goldstein, Irwin. 2002. 'Are Emotions Feelings? A Further Look at Hedonic Theories of Emotion' in *Consciousness and Emotion*. 3 (1): 21-33.

Gombrich, Ernest H. 1975. *Art History and Social Sciences*. The Romanes Lecture for 1973. Oxford: Clarendon Press.

--. 1995. *The Story of Art*. London: Phaidon Press.

Greenfield, Patricia M. (2000). 'Three Approaches to the Psychology of Culture: where do they come from? Where can they go?' in *Asian Journal of Social Psychology*. 3: 223-240

Griffiths, Paul E. 1998. 'Emotions' in Bechtel, G. and Graham, G. (eds). A Companion to Cognitive Science. Oxford: Blackwell.

Grodal, Torben. 1997. *Moving Pictures: a New Theory of Film Genres, Feelings, and Cognition.* Oxford: Clarendon Press.

--. 2003. *Filmopplevelse – en Indføring i Audiovisuel Teori og Analyse.* Fredriksberg: Forlagets Samfundslitteratur.

Heidegger, Martin. 2003. *Kunstværkets Oprindelse.* Gyldendal. 1935.

Helles, Rasmus and Køppe, Simo. 1999. 'Æstetikken der Forsvandt' in *Kritik* 140:61-72.

Hillman, James. 1960. *Emotion.* London: Routledge and Keagan Paul.

Hjort, Mette and Laver, Sue (eds). 1997. *Emotions and the Arts.* Oxford: Oxford University Press.

James, William. 1983. *The Principles of Psychology.* Cambridge: Harvard University Press. 1893.

--. 1884. 'What is an Emotion?' in *Mind*, 9 (34), 188-205

--. 1929. *The Varieties of Religious Experience.* New York: Modern Library Books. 1902.

Johnson, Mark. 1987. *The Body in the Mind. The Bodily Basis of Meaning, Imagination and Reason.* Chicago: The University of Chicago Press.

Joseph, Jonathan and Roberts, John M. (eds). 2004. *Realism, Discourse and Deconstruction.* London: Routledge

Joy, Annamma and Sherry, John F. 2003. 'Speaking of Art as Embodied Imagination: a Multisensory Approach to Understanding Aesthetic Experience' in *Journal of Consumer Research.* 30(2): 259-282.

Jørgensen, Per. S. 1989. 'Om Kvalitative Analyser og deres Gyldighed' in *Nordisk Psykologi.* 41(1): 25-41

Kant, Immanuel. 1997. *Critique of Judgement.* (tr. J.C. Meredith). Oxford University Press. 1790.

Kazdin, A.E. (editor in chief). 2000. *Encyclopaedia of Psychology.* Washington, D.C.: American Psychological Association

Kennedy, M..M. 1979. 'Generalizing from Single Case Studies' in *Evaluation Quarterly.* 3: 661-678.

Kim, Jaegwon. 1996. *Philosophy of Mind.* Boulder, Colorado: Westview Press

Kitayama, Shinobu and Markus, Hazel R. (eds). 1994. *Emotion and Culture: Empirical Studies of Mutual Influence.* Washington, DC: American Psychological Association.

Kjørup, Søren. 2000. *Kunstens Filosofi – en Indføring i Aestetik.* Roskilde Universitets Forlag.

Kripke, Saul A. 1982. *Naming and Necessity.* Harvard University Press.

Kvale, Steinar. 1992. 'Introduction: From the Archaeology of the Psyche to the Architecture of Cultural Landscapes' in Kvale, S. (ed.) *Psychology and Postmodernism.* London: Sage Publications: 1-16.

--. 1997. *InterView: en Introduktion til det Kvalitative Forskningsinterview.* Hans Reitzels Forlag.

Kövecses, Zoltan. 2000. *Metaphor and Emotion. Language, Culture and Body in Human Feeling.* Cambridge: Cambridge University Press

Lakoff, George. 1987. *Women, Fire and Dangerous Things. What Categories Reveal About the Mind.* Chicago and London: University of Chicago Press.

Lakoff, George and Johnson, Mark. 1980. *Metaphors we live by.* Chicago and London: Chicago University Press.

Lakoff, George and Johnson, Mark. 1999. *Philosophy in the Flesh. The Embodied Mind and its Challenge to Western Thought.* New York: Basic Books

Lazarus, Richard S. 1982. 'Thoughts on the Relations between Emotion and Cognition' in *American Psychologist,* 37 (9): 1019-1024.

--. 1984. 'On the Primacy of Cognition' in *American Psychologist,* 39, 124-129.

--. 1991. *Emotion and Adaptation.* New York: Oxford University Press.

--. 1999. 'The Cognition-Emotion Debate: a Bit of History' in Dalgleish, T. and Power, M. (eds). *Handbook of Cognition and Emotion.* New York: John Wiley & Sons: 3-20.

LeDoux, Joseph. 1998. *The Emotional Brain. The Mysterious Underpinnings of Emotional life.* New York: Simon and Schuster

--. 2002. *Synaptic Self. How our Brains become who we are.* Viking Penguin.

Leventhal, H and Scherer, K 1987. 'The Relationship of Emotion to Cognition: a Functional Approach to a Semantic Controversy' in *Cognition and Emotion.* 1: 3-28.

Levine, Joseph. 1983. 'Materialism and Qualia: the Explanatory Gap' in *Pacific Philosophical Quarterly* 64: 354-61.

--. 1997. 'On leaving out what it's like' in Block, N. J., Flanagan O., Guzeldere G. (Eds.) *The Nature of Consciousness. Philosophical debates.* Cambridge, Mass.: MIT Press: 543-555.

Levinson, Jerrold. 1997. 'Emotion in Response to Art: a Survey of the Terrain' in Hjort, M. and Laver, S. (eds). *Emotions and the Arts.* Oxford: Oxford University Press: 20-34.

Levi-Strauss, Claude 1995. *Den Vilde Tanke.* København: Samlerens Bogklub. 1962.

Loewenstein, George and Lerner, Jennifer S. 2003. 'The Role of Affect in Decision-making' in Davidson, Scherer, and Goldsmith (eds). *Handbook of Affective Sciences.* Oxford: Oxford University Press: 618-642

MacDonald, Cynthia and MacDonald, Graham (eds). 1995. *Philosophy of Psychology.* Oxford: Blackwell.

Marr, David. 1982. *A Computational Investigation into the Human Representation and Processing of Visual Information.* New York: Freeman

Martindale, Colin. 1999. 'Peak Shift, Prototypicality and Aesthetic Preference' in *Journal of Consciousness Studies.* 6: 52-54.

Matravers, Derek. 1998. *Art and Emotion.* New York: Oxford University Press.

Mayne, Tracy J. and Bonanno, George A. 2001. *Emotions: Current Issues and Future Directions.* New York: Guilford Press

McAdams, Dan P. 1996. 'Personality, Modernity, and the Storied Self: A Contemporary Framework for Studying Persons' in *Psychological Inquiry* 7(4): 295-321.

McGinn, Colin. 1989 'Can We Solve the Mind-Body problem?' in *Mind.* 98 (391): 349-366.

Merleau-Ponty, Maurice. 1962. *Phenomenology of Perception.* London: Routledge & Keagan Paul. 1945.

Mitter P. 1999. 'A Short Commentary on "the Science of Art"' in *Journal of Consciousness Studies.* 6: 64-65.

Nagel, Thomas. 1991. 'What Is It Like to Be a Bat?' in Rosenthal, D.M. (ed.). *The Nature of Mind.* Oxford University Press: 422-428. 1974.

Nagel, Thomas. 2000. 'The Psychophysical Nexus' in Boghossian and Peacocke (eds.). *New Essays on the A Priori.* Oxford: Clarendon Press: 432-471

Norris, Christopher. 2004. 'Deconstructing anti-realism: Derrida's 'White Mythology'' in Joseph, Jonathan and Roberts, John M. (eds). *Realism Discourse and Deconstruction.* London: Routledge: 262-297

Nussbaum, Martha C. 2001. *Upheavals of Thought. The Intelligence of Emotion.* Cambridge University Press.

Olsen, Henning. 2002. 'Kvaler eller Kvalitet? En Evaluering af Danske Kvalitative Interviewundersøgelser' in *Nordisk Psykologi* 54: 145-172.

Panksepp, Jaak. 2003. 'At the Interface of the Affective, Behavioural, and Cognitive Neurosciences: Decoding the Emotional Feelings of the Brain' in *Brain and Cognition* 52: 4-14.

Parsons, Michael J. 1987. *How we understand Art: a Cognitive Developmental Account of Aesthetic Experience.* Cambridge: Cambridge University Press.

Phan, K. K., Wagner, T, Stephan F. T. and Liberzon, I. 2002. 'Functional Neuroanatomy of Emotion: A Meta-analysis of Emotion Activation Studies in PET and fMRI' in *NeuroImage.* 16(2): 331-348.

Pizzagalli, D., Shackman, A. J. and Davidson, R. J. 2003. 'The Functional Neuroimaging of Human Emotion: Asymmetric Contributions of Cortical and Subcortical Circuitry' in Hugdahl, K. and Davidson, R. J. (Eds). *The Asymmetrical brain.* Cambridge, Mass: MIT Press: 511-532

Plutchik, Robert. 1994. *The Psychology and Biology of Emotion.* New York: Harper Collins College Publishers.

Plutchik, Robert. 2000. *Emotions in the Practice of Psychotherapy: Clinical Implications of Affect Theories.* Washington, DC: American Psychological Association.

Polkinghorne, Donald E. 1992. 'Postmodern Epistemology of Practice' in Kvale, S. (ed.). *Psychology and Postmodernism.* London: Sage Publications: 146-165.

Power, Mick and Dalgleish, Tim. 1997. *Cognition and Emotion. From Order to Disorder*. East Sussex: Psychology Press Publishers.

Putnam, Hillary 1975. *Mind, Language and Reality. Philosophical Papers vol. 2*. Cambridge: Cambridge University Press: 240-249. 1967

Ramachandran V. and Hirstein W. 1999. 'The Science of art. A Neurological Theory of Aesthetic Experience' in *Journal of Consciousness Studies* 6: 15-51

Reisenzein, R. and Schönpflug, W. 1992. 'Stumpf's Cognitive-evaluative Theory of Emotion' in *American Psychologist* 47(1): 34-45.

Roget, P. M. 2000. *Roget's Thesaurus of English Words and Phrases*. London: Penguin Books. 1852.

Rorty, Richard. 1989. *Philosophy and the Mirror of Nature*. Oxford: Basil Blackwell. 1980.

Salmela, Mikko. 2002. 'The Problem of Affectivity in Cognitive Theories of Emotions' in *Consciousness and Emotion* 3(2): 159-182

Sartre Jean-Poul. 1988. *The Transcendence of the Ego: An Existentialist Theory of Consciousness*. Farrar, Straus and Giroux. 1937.

--. 1984. *Being and Nothingness. A Phenomenological Essay on Ontology*. New York: Washington Square Press. 1943.

Schachter, S. and Singer, J.E. 1962. 'Cognitive, Social and Physiological Determinants of Emotional State' in *Psychological Review*. 69: 379-399.

Scherer, Klaus R. 2000. 'Psychological Models of Emotion' in Borod, J. C. (Ed.). *The Neuropsychology of Emotion. Series in Affective Science*. London: Oxford University Press. 137-162.

Shanon B. 1993. *The Representational and Presentational. An Essay on Cognition and the Study of Mind*. Hemel Hempstead: Harvester Wheatsheaf.

Simpson, J.A. and Weiner, E.S.C (general eds). 1994. Oxford English Dictionary, the Complete Version. Oxford: Oxford University Press.

Sorabji, Richard. 2000. *Emotion and Peace of Mind. From Stoic Agitation to Christian Temptation*. Oxford: Oxford University Press.

Spinelli, Ernesto. 1989. *The Interpreted World. An Introduction to Phenomenological Psychology*. London: Sage publications.

Strauss, Ansel og Corbin, Juliet. 1994. *Basics of Qualitative Research Techniques and Procedures for Developing Grounded Theory*. Sage Publications.

Strongman, K. T. 2003. *The Psychology of Emotion. From Everyday Life to Theory*. West Sussex: John Wiley and Sons, Ltd.

Teasdale John D. 1999. 'Multi-level Theories of Cognition-emotion Relations' in Dalgleish, T. and Power, M.J. (eds). *Handbook of Cognition and Emotion*. West Sussex: John Wiley and Sons, Ltd. 637-681.

Turnbull, O. H., Berry, H., Bowman, C. H. 2003. 'Direct versus indirect Emotional Consequences of the Iowa Gambling Task' in *Brain and Cognition* 53(2): 389-392.

Vinterberg, Hermann and Bodelsen C. A. 1966. *Danish to English Dictionary*. Copenhagen: Nordisk Forlag.

Wierzbicka. 1994. 'Emotion, Language and Cultural Scripts' in Kitayama, S. and Markus, H. R. (Eds). *Emotion and Culture: Empirical Studies of Mutual Influence*. Washington, DC: American Psychological Association: 133-196

Wittgenstein, Ludvig. 1958. *Philosophical Investigations*. 3rd. edition. London: Macmillian. 1945.

Woodfield, Richard. 1999. 'Book review of The Psychology of Art Appreciation'. *British Journal of Aesthetics*. 39: 207-209.

Wright, Kathleen. 1998. 'Gadamer' in Craig, Edward (general ed.) *Routledge Encyclopedia of Philosophy*. Version 1.0. Routledge.

Zahavi, Dan. 2001. *Husserls Fænomenologi*. Gyldendal.

Zajonc Robert B. 1980. 'Feeling and Thinking: Preferences Need No Inferences' in *American Psychologist*. 35, 151-175.

--. 1984. 'On the Primacy of Affect' in *American Psychologist*, 39(2): 117-123

--. 2000. 'Feeling and Thinking: closing the Debate over the Independence of Affect' in Forgas, J. P. (ed.). *Feeling and Thinking: the Role of Affect in Social Cognition*. Cambridge University Press: 31-59.

Zeki, Semir. 1999. 'Art and the Brain' in *Journal of Counsciousness Studies*. 6: 76-96.

Index

www.ingramcontent.com/pod-product-compliance
Lightning Source LLC
Chambersburg PA
CBHW072145020426
42334CB00018B/1893